Time for HOMEWORK

Paul
Nightingale

1

Book 1

Hunter Education Nightingale

HUNTER
EDUCATION
NIGHTINGALE

Copyright © 2015 Paul Nightingale
Time for Homework - Book 1

Published by:
Hunter Education Nightingale
ABN: 69 055 798 626
PO Box 547
Warners Bay NSW 2282
Ph: 0417 658 777
email: sales@huntereducationnightingale.com.au
paul@huntereducationnightingale.com.au
www.huntereducationnightingale.com.au

Cover Design: Doriana Berkovic

National Library of Australia Card No.
and ISBN 978 - 1 - 922242 - 25 - 9

COPYRIGHT

This book is copyright. Except as permitted under the Copyright Act, for example any fair dealing for the purposes of private study, research, criticism or review, no part of this book may be reproduced, stored in retrieval system, or transmitted in any form or by any means without prior permission. All enquiries should be made to the publisher.

COPYING FOR EDUCATIONAL PURPOSES

The Copyright Act allows a maximum of one chapter or 10% of this book, whichever is greater, to be copied by any educational institution for its educational purposes provided that the educational institution has given a remuneration notice to Copyright Agency Limited ('CAL') under the Copyright Act or there is a licence agreement between CAL and that educational institution (e.g. Department of Education).

In the absence of such an agreement or a remuneration notice, an educational institution must seek written permission for any copying from the copyright owner, or its exclusive licensee, and make payment, when requested. All inquiries should be made to the publisher.

For details of the CAL licence for educational institutions or which educational institutions can give CAL a remuneration notice, contact CAL, Level 15, 233 Castlereagh Street, Sydney, NSW 2000. Telephone (02) 9394 7600.

RECYCLING

When the program is completed and the paper no longer wanted, be sure to have it recycled.
The time and care taken to recycle may help save a tree and maintain our environment.

Time for Homework
Book 1

Time for Homework Book 1 is the second in a series of seven books written to help reinforce many of the concepts, skills and understanding needed with today's school curriculum. The series is designed as a user friendly resource that treats reading, handwriting, spelling, grammar, writing and mathematics.

The book contains 30 units of work. Each unit can be attempted over the period of one week. Each unit addresses the subjects outlined above along with topics addressed in today's environment and those in the new Australian Curriculum for Mathematics and English.

As the child's skills develop with sounds, words and reading the book introduces stories and rhymes. Rhymes are key learning techniques that are catchy to the ear of the child. They help in the development of word families and an understanding of written texts. In addition the child is introduced to comprehension, punctuation and some grammar. At all times there is an emphasis on spelling and word association.

While *Time for Homework* treats many of the topics presented in the school curriculum, it is a summary of those subjects. This book is fun to use at home for the child. *Time for Homework* is a resource that will help develop learning.

Message to Parents

With *Time for Homework Book 1* you may need to help with some reading instructions. As a parent you are asked to help with this skill, but please resist the temptation to actually provide answers. Help with explanation, where necessary and assist when needed. As your child works through the book your help will be required less. Reading, maths, handwriting spelling skills, grammar and knowledge of English will develop allowing the child to become a more independent learner with an understanding of the topics treated.

Regular homework helps develop skills in the subject areas treated and confidence in your child with learning which is essential for a good education.

Praise your child at all times, because you are the ideal support person in your child's life. Working together will help with the use of this book. It will help make the learning process more meaningful for you both. *Time for Homework Book 1* is designed as a fun book to use at home. Enjoy the journey!

Read the rhyme.

Today is Wednesday and I am at school.

This afternoon I will swim in the pool.

Tomorrow is Thursday, mum cooks chops.

Before she can she visits the shops.

Write words from the poem that rhyme with.

school ______________ shops ______________

Complete the stories.

Mum buys the chops from school. / shops.

In the afternoon I can swim. / go to school.

What day comes after Thursday? ___________

Word Families

Add the **'at'** sound to the each letter to label the pictures.

at

h___ ___ m___ ___

c___ ___ b___ ___

r___ ___

Spelling

Read, trace over and copy these words.
Write each word again.

		copy	write
today	today	____________	____________
mum	mum	____________	____________
she	she	____________	____________
swim	swim	____________	____________

Punctuation

Add capital letters, full stops.

☐y mum likes to cook cakes○

☐n ☐riday we eat fish for dinner ○

Number

Write the number of dots on each domino.

a. 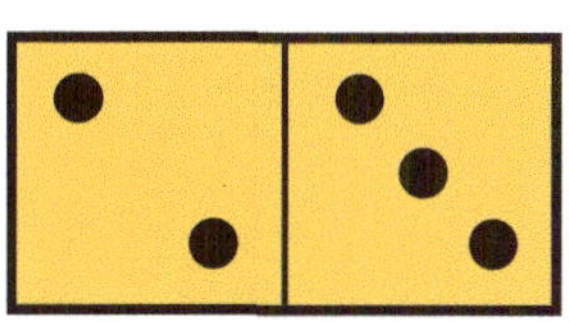 ☐ ☐

b. 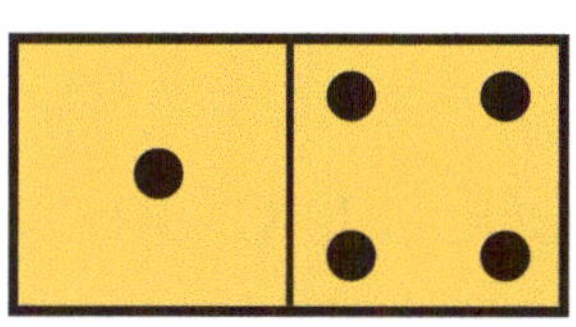 ☐ ☐

c.  ☐ ☐

d. 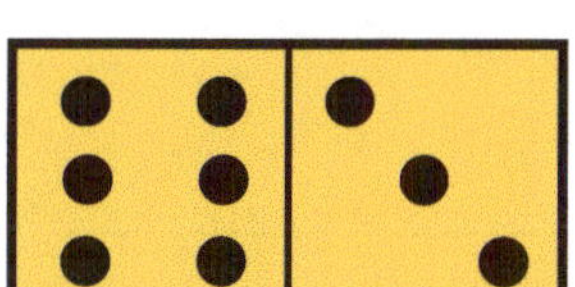 ☐ ☐

Time

Draw a line to where days of the week belong.

____

Tuesday

Wednesday

____

Friday

____

Sunday

Thursday

Saturday

Monday

Read the rhyme.

Yesterday was my birthday, I was six.
Mum cooked a cake I helped to mix.
She baked it in the oven, then iced it on top.
With six pink candles that came from the shop.

Write words from the poem that rhyme with.

mix ______________ top ______________

Complete the story paths.

I helped mum (cook / mix) the cake.

It was my birthday and I was (six. / seven.)

How old are you? __________

Word Families

Add the letters to make **'et'** words.

b	_et	_et	**s**
l	_et	_et	**p**
w	_et	_et	**v**
j	_et	_et	**n**
g	_et	_et	**m**

Spelling

Unjumble the letters to label each picture.

kaec __________

umm __________

tne __________

Read, trace over and copy these words.
Write each word again.

		copy	write
shop	shop		
girl	girl		
dad	dad		
cake	cake		

Write words from the list that match these outlines.

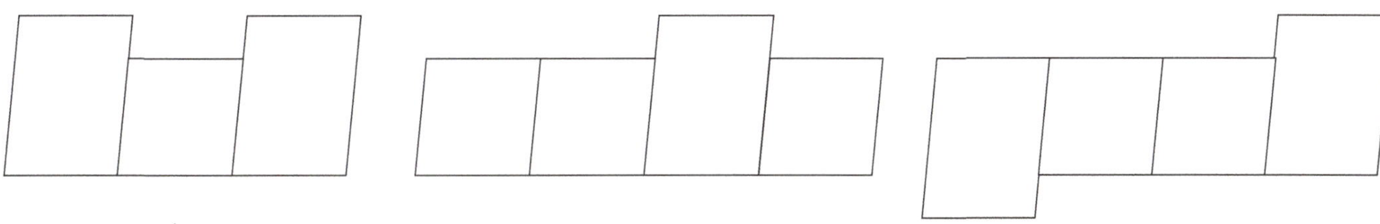

Addition

1. Add numbers on the number lines.
Fill in the number sentences.

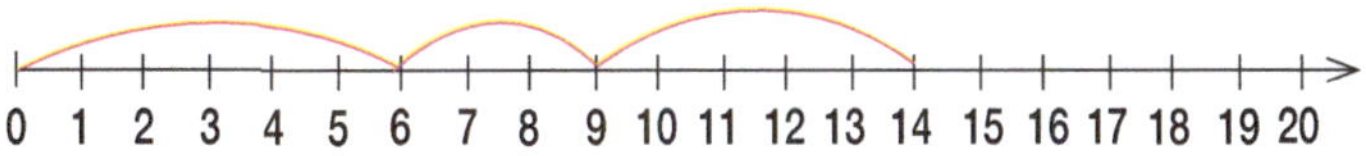

☐ and ☐ and ☐ make ☐

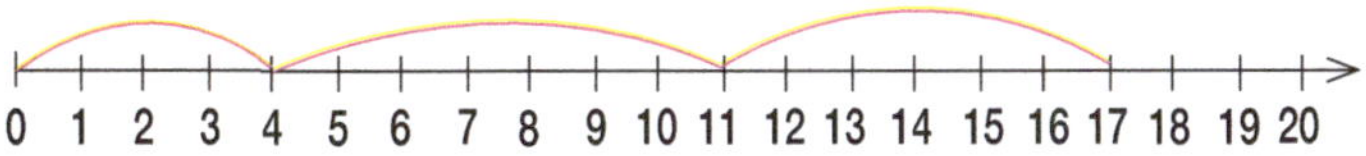

☐ and ☐ and ☐ make ☐

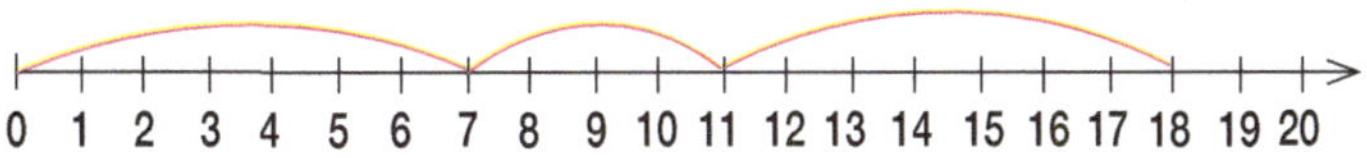

☐ and ☐ and ☐ make ☐

Length

2. Tick the objects longer than a ruler. ☑

Reading

Read the months of the year.

January	February	March	April	May
June	July	August	September	
October	November	December		

- Colour the month that you have your birthday.
- Write the month it is now. ____________________
- Write the day it is today. ____________________
- Count the number of months in the year, then write the total. [ ]

Word Families

Add the '**op**' sound to each letter to label the pictures.

t_____

m_____

st_____

sh_____

Spelling

Unjumble the letters to label the pictures.

yabb ________

ybo ________

oct ________

ablonol ________

ihsf ________

Handwriting

Trace over capital and lower case '**L l**'. Copy the sentence.

Trace L L L

l l l

Look at the little lady.

Copy ____________________

Read, trace over and copy the words.

		copy	write
fish	fish		
boy	boy		
school	school		
day	day		

Write words from the list that fit these outlines.

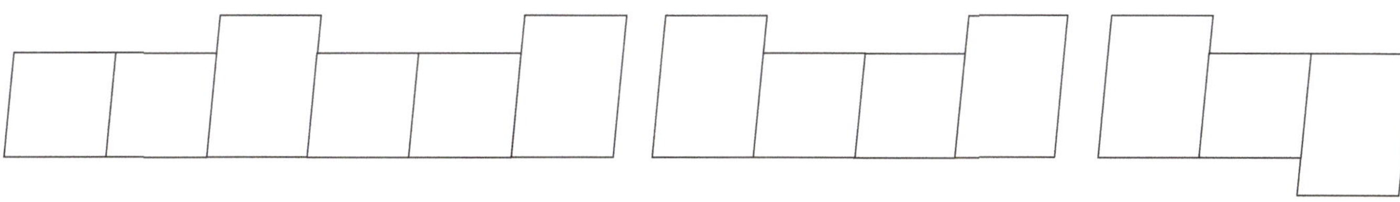

Time

1. What's the time?

a.  ☐ o'clock

b. 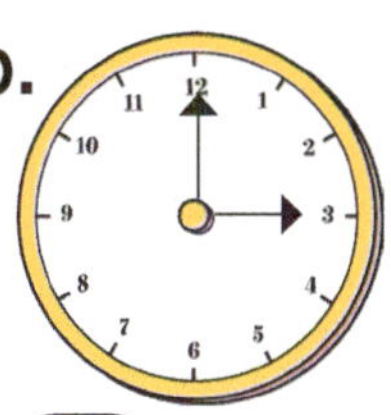 ☐ o'clock

c. 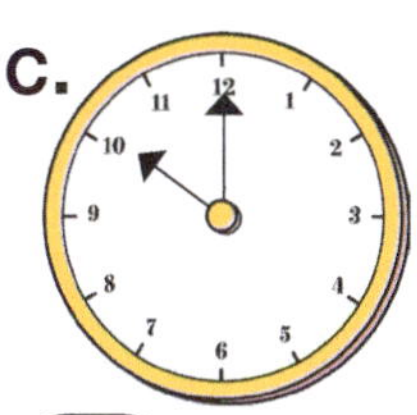 ☐ o'clock

2. Match the digital and analogue clocks that show the same time.

a. 2:00 b. 8:00 c. 4:00

d. 

e. 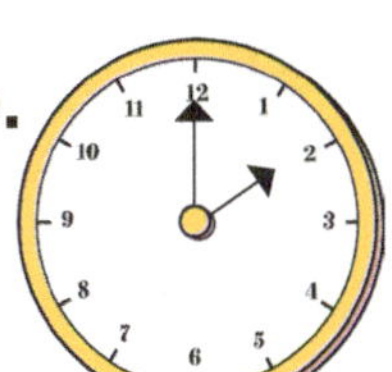

f. 

Mass

3. Tick the one in each group that is **heavier**. ☑

a.  ☐ ☐

b.  ☐ ☐

4. Order the mass of these objects from **lightest** to **heaviest**. 1-6.

a.  ☐

b.  ☐

c.  ☐

d.  ☐

e. 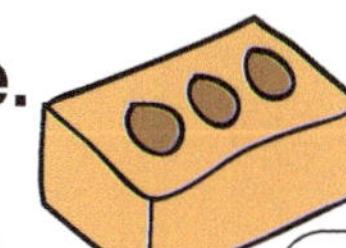 ☐

f.  ☐

Read the rhyme.

Baa, baa, black sheep,
Have you any wool?
Yes sir, yes sir,
Three bags full.
One for the master,
One for the dame,
And one for the little boy,
who lives down the lane.

- Did the sheep have any wool? ☐ Yes ☐ No
- How many bags of wool? ☐ bags of wool.
- Did the little boy get any wool? ☐ Yes ☐ No
- How many bags did the little boy get? ☐

Vocabulary

Add letters to write words from the poem.

b s y l d w t o

__ool	__heep
__oy	__hree
__ittle	__es
__ne	__own

Spelling

Unjumble the letters to label the pictures.

gpi

____

gba

____

reteh

____

rca

____

tage

____

Read the words. Trace over the letters, then copy and write each word.

		copy	write
little	little		
big	big		
yes	yes		
gate	gate		

Write words from the list that fit these outlines.

Capacity

1. Tick the one that will hold the **most** in each group. ☑

a.

b.

c.

Take Away

2. Count each group then take away those **'crossed off'**. Fill in the sentence.

a.

☐ take away ☐ leaves ☐

b.

☐ take away ☐ leaves ☐

c.

☐ take away ☐ leaves ☐

Read the description about the weather.

Summer, winter, autumn, spring
Are the seasons that always bring
The rain, wind, sun and snow.
These all help flowers grow.

- Write what the seasons bring. ________ ________ ________ ________
- Write the season before summer. ____________________

Writing

Colour story paths to write a sentence.

warm | It is | cold
sunny | hot | raining
today. It is
cloudy
outside.

Word Building

Add the starting letters to write **'it'** words.

__it
__it
__it
__it

s h l m
b f k p
w

__it
__it
__it
__it
__it

Spelling

Unjumble the letters to label the pictures.

owlfres

____

inra

____

oculsd

____

Read the words. Trace over each word, then copy and write each word again.

words	trace	copy	write
wind	wind		
rain	rain		
always	always		
spring	spring		
flowers	flowers		

Write words from the list or description that fit these outlines.

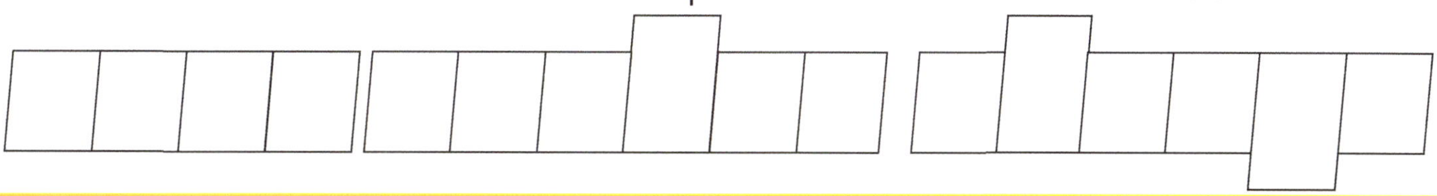

Number

Match the matches to the numbers.

a. 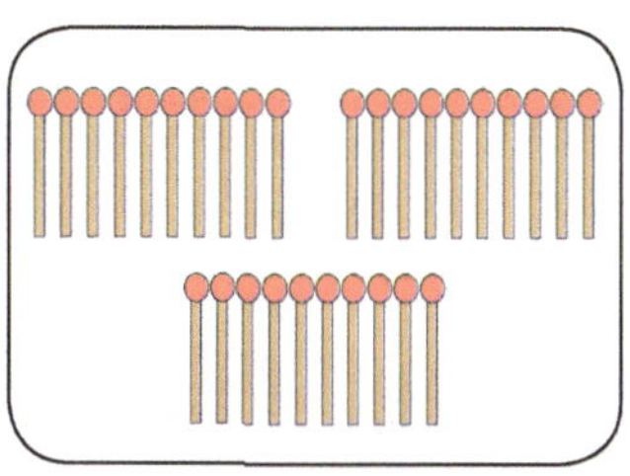

b. 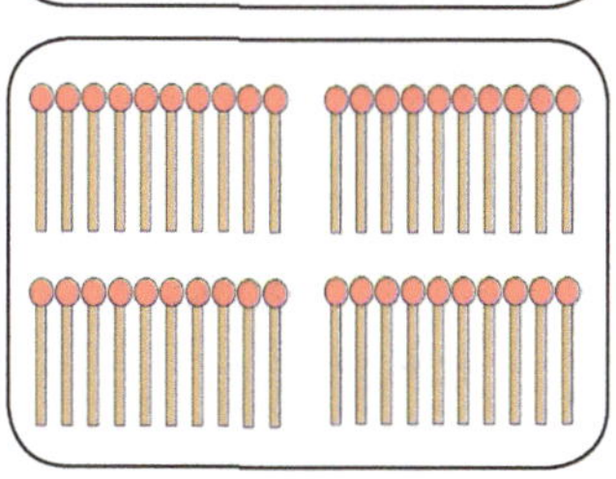

c. 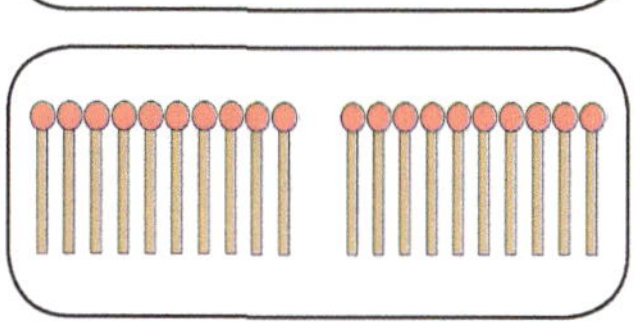

d. 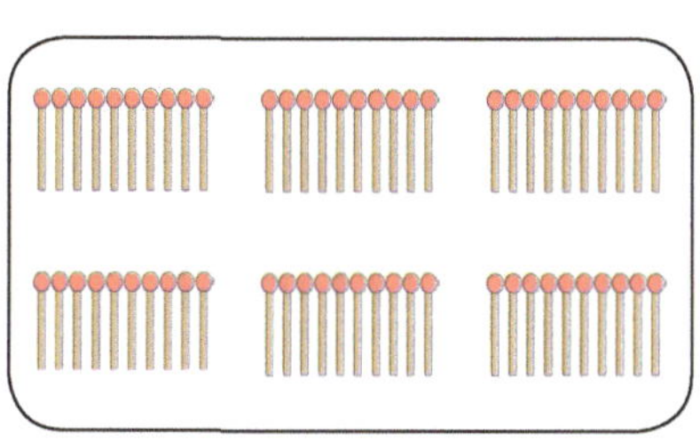

20

60

30

40

Numbers

Match words to the correct number.

sixty

fourty

ninety

seventy

fifty

20

40

70

50

80

60

90

30

100

10

thirty

twenty

one hundred

ten

eighty

Read the story, then complete the activities.

My sister and I have a dog, a cat and a turtle at home. Every afternoon we feed our pets. Sometimes our little dog Scruffy tries to eat the cat food. Molly, the cat, hisses and her tail goes all fluffy. Speedy, the turtle just likes to eat lettuce and cabbage leaves.

Understanding

Draw lines to make sentences.

We have a dog	that likes to eat leaves.
Molly is the name	cat and turtle at home.
Speedy is a turtle	the cat food.
Scruffy tries to eat	of our cat.

Interpreting

Colour the bubble that fits the best answers.

The animals are fed ◯ in the morning. ◯ every afternoon.

Speedy is a ◯ cat. ◯ turtle. ◯ dog.

Word Building

__ap

__ap

__ap

__an

__ap

__an

Spelling

Unjumble the letters to label the pictures.

ofdo ____________

rultte ____________

telceut ____________

fffylu ____________

Read the words. Trace over the letters, then copy and write each word.

words	trace	copy	write
afternoon	afternoon	____________	____________
tail	tail	____________	____________
every	every	____________	____________
each	each	____________	____________
like	like	____________	____________

Write words from the list or story that fit these outlines.

Money

Match the coins to their names.

five cents

ten cents

twenty cents

fifty cents

one dollar

two dollars

Numbers

Here is a graph about fruit.

- Write how many of each fruit.
- Which fruit was most popular?

____

- Which fruit totalled the same?

____

- How much fruit in total?

Read the poem.

Chickens, chickens everywhere
Some on the ground and some on a chair.
Chickens, chickens chirp a lot.
Mum cooks ours in a pot.
Chickens, chickens oh so many.
My pet chicken is called Henny Penny.

Understanding Draw a line to make sentences.

Some chickens are on	my pet chicken.
Henny Penny is	chickens everywhere.
Mum cooks chicken	a chair.
There are lots of	in a pot.

Interpreting Colour the bubble that fits the best answers.

Chickens like to ◯ be cooked. ◯ chirp a lot.
Mum cooks chicken ◯ in a pot. ◯ on a chair.

Word Building

Add the blending sound '**ch**' to label pictures and write the words.

__ __icken

__ __ildren

__ __ips

__ __air

__ __ur __ __

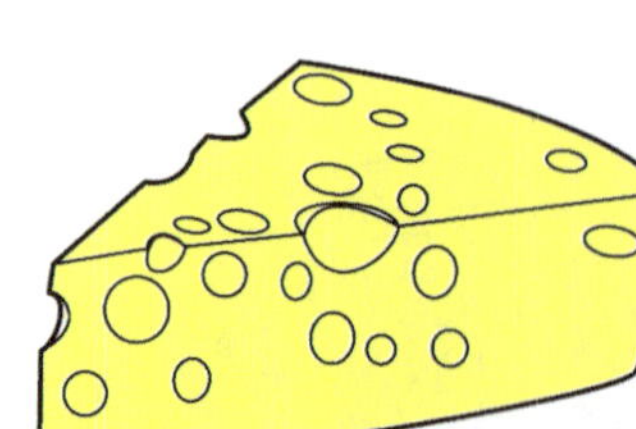

__ __eese

Read the words. Trace over the letters, then copy and write each word.

words	trace	copy	write
chair	chair		
chirp	chirp		
church	church		
chips	chips		
children	children		

Write words from the list or poem that fit these outlines.

2D Shapes

Match shapes to their names.

hexagon

triangle

circle

rectangle

pentagon

square

Fractions

Colour half of each item or group.

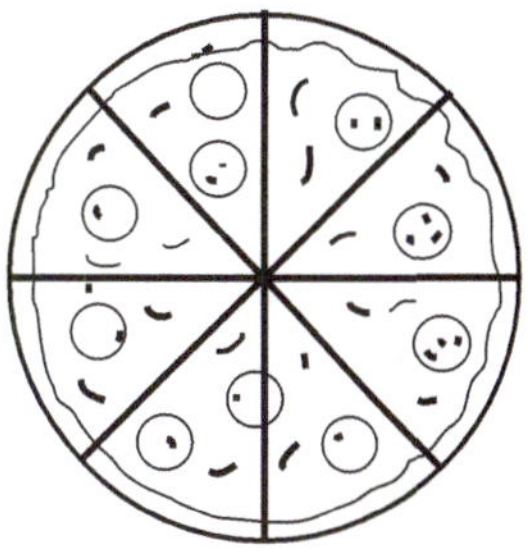

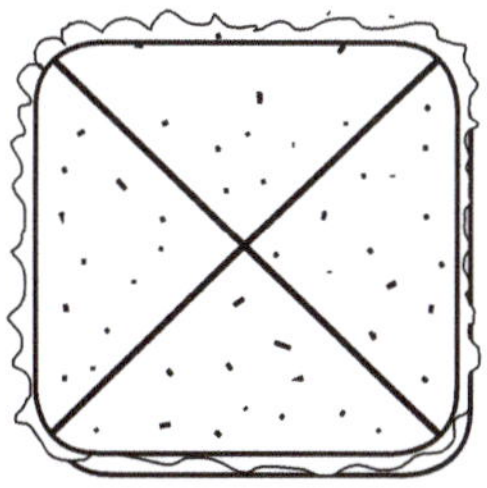

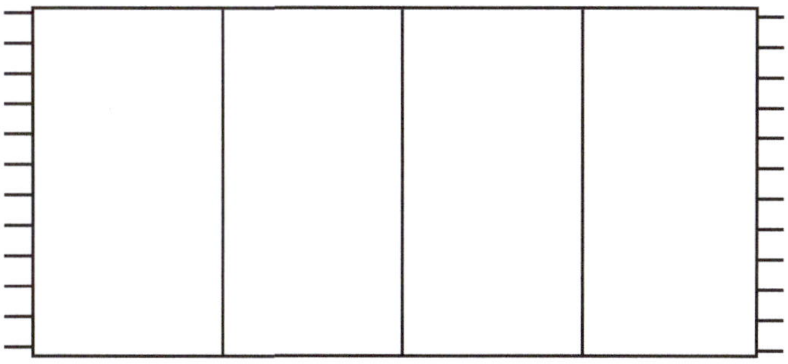

Reading — Unit 8

Read the story, then complete the activities.

Mum took me to the shoe shop to get new shoes for school. My old shoes had worn out with the heel lifting. The shoe man said my feet had grown since last year. He remembered mum and me. Mum said she had to get shoes for Shelley, my sister too. She is in Year 6.

Understanding

Draw a line to make sentences.

My old shoes	buy shoes.
Mum took me to	my feet had grown.
Shelley needed	had worn out.
The shoe man said	shoes too.

Interpreting

Colour the bubble that best fits the answers.

All children's feet ◯ need shoes. ◯ grow every year.

The shoe man has ◯ a good memory. ◯ knows my sister.

Word Building

Add the sound **'sh'** to label pictures.

__ __oe

__ __ip

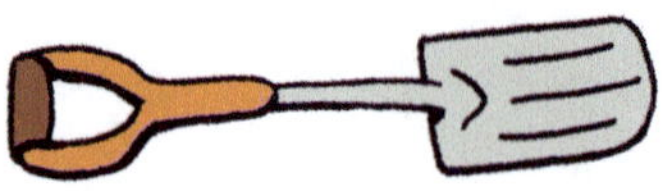

__ __ovel

__ __irt

Handwriting

Trace over the capital and lower case letters. Copy the words.

T T T t t t t

tilt little Lit

Read the words. Trace over letters, then copy and write each word.

words	trace	copy	write
shop	shop		
shine	shine		
shirt	shirt		
shake	shake		
said	said		

Write words from the list or story that fit these outlines.

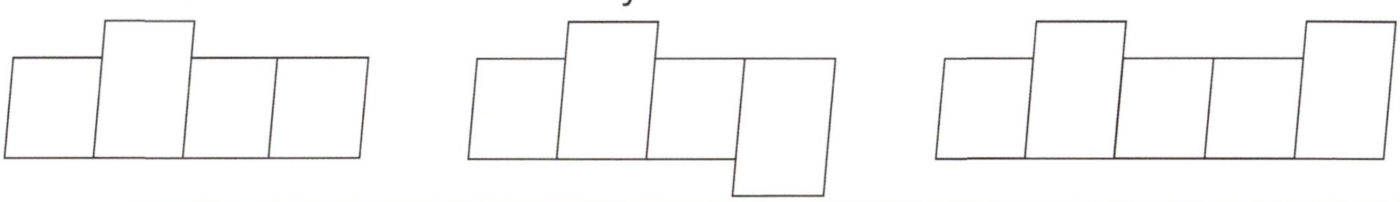

3D Shapes

Match solids to their names.

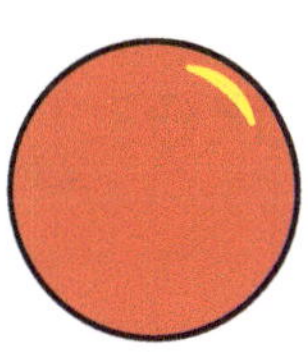

cone

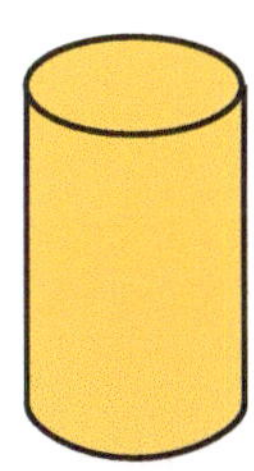

pyramid

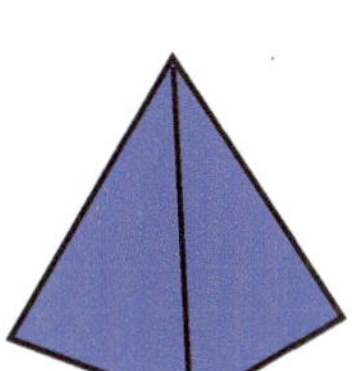

cube

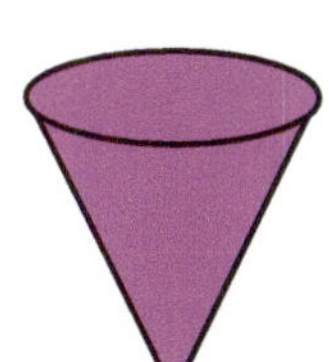

sphere

prism

cylinder

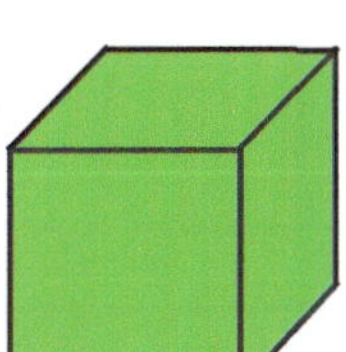

Chance

Colour the pictures of what **could happen** tomorrow.

a. 

b. 

c. 

d. 

e. 

Reading

Read the story about food, then complete the activities.

Eating good food helps to keep us healthy. I like to eat good food. It is fun when it is time for desserts. Cakes and biscuits are also fun but I like cream buns best. Fruits, vegetables, meats and bread all help to keep us healthy. What foods do you like best? Draw them.

My favourite foods.

Understanding

Draw a line to make sentences.

Eating good food	is a cream bun.
Fun foods I like to eat are	helps keep us healthy.
The food I like best	biscuits and cakes.

Handwriting

Trace over the capital and lower case letters. Copy the sentence.

trace A A A A

trace a a a a

trace D D D D

trace d d d d

All dads like to dance all day.

copy

Read the words. Trace over letters, then copy and write each word.

words	trace	copy	write
help	help	______	______
food	food	______	______
cake	cake	______	______
good	good	______	______
bread	bread	______	______

Write words from the list that fit these frames.

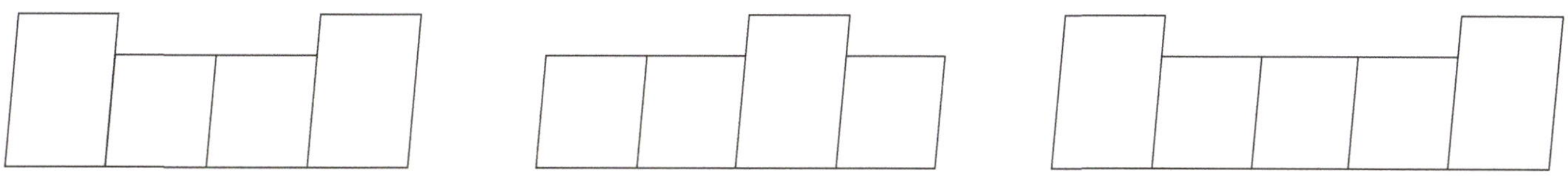

Place Value

1. Write the number shown on each abacus.

a. 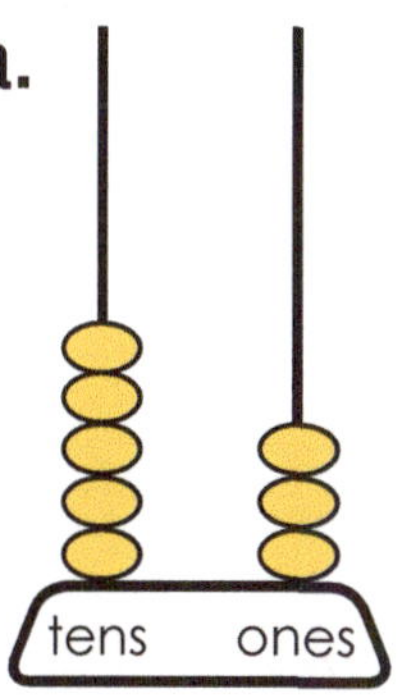

b. 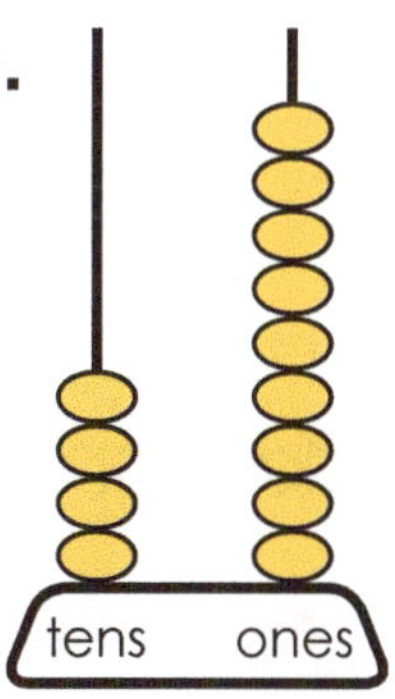

c. 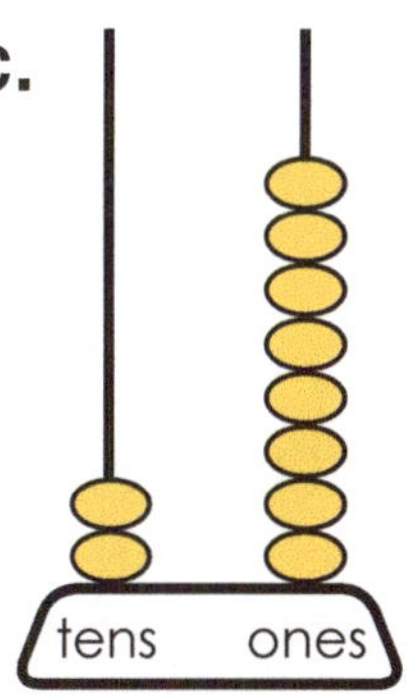

______ ______ ______

2. Write the number shown on each place value card.

a. 8 tens 5 ones = ☐

b. 7 tens 4 ones = ☐

Addition

1. Write how many dots on each domino, then add them together.

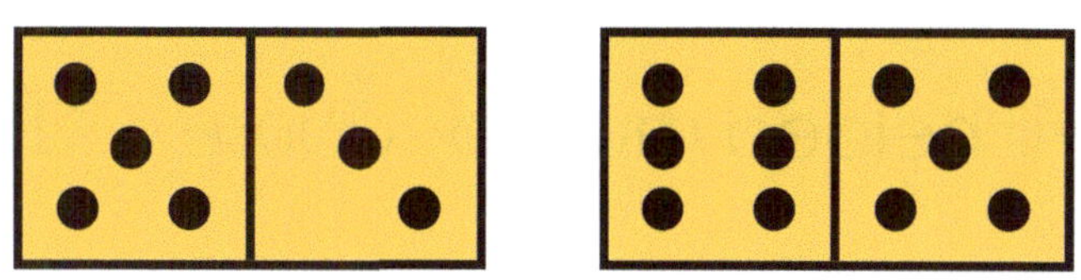

☐ + ☐ = ☐ ☐ + ☐ = ☐

2. Count each group of counters, then add the groups.

a. 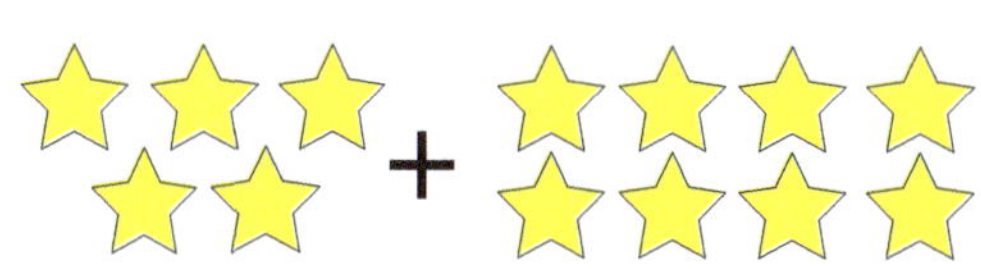

☐ + ☐ = ☐

b. 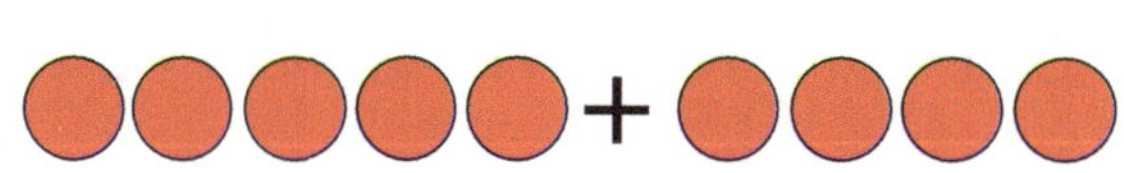

☐ + ☐ = ☐

Reading

Read the story. Complete story activities.

Last Sunday afternoon, Will helped his mum clean the house. They washed all the floors, first. Then they made the beds. Mum said that Will was a good helper.

Later, mum and Will made lunch. Will liked food so he was happy to help. When they washed the dishes, mum told Will he could go and play outside. Mum said, next time Will was 'grounded' he would do more cleaning.

Understanding

Draw a line to make sentences.

First, mum and Will	because he liked food.
Will was happy to make lunch	last Sunday afternoon.
Will was grounded	washed the floors.

Interpreting

Colour the bubble that best fits the story.

Will helped mum because ○ he was grounded. ○ he liked food.

Next time Will is grounded
- ○ he will do more cleaning.
- ○ he will make lunch.

Punctuation

Rewrite the sentences, adding capital letters and full stops.

- will was grounded last sunday afternoon

___

- on sunday will and paris went to sydney

___

Spelling

Read the words. Trace over letters, then copy and write each word.

words	trace	copy	write
lunch	lunch		
made	made		
dish	dish		
happy	happy		
help	help		

Write words from the list or story that fit these frames.

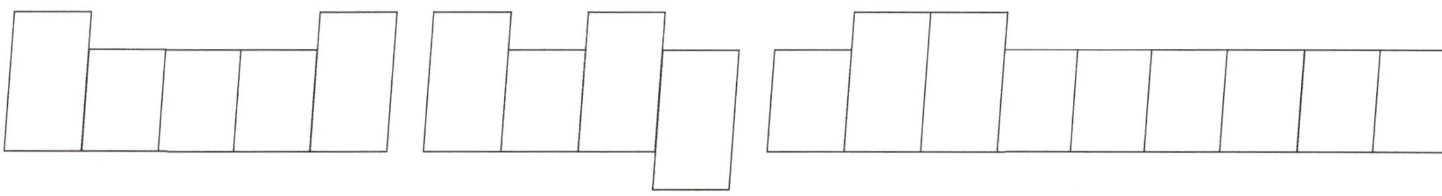

Odd and Even Numbers

Colour the jumpers with odd numbers.

Subtraction

1. Count the groups, then subtract.

a. 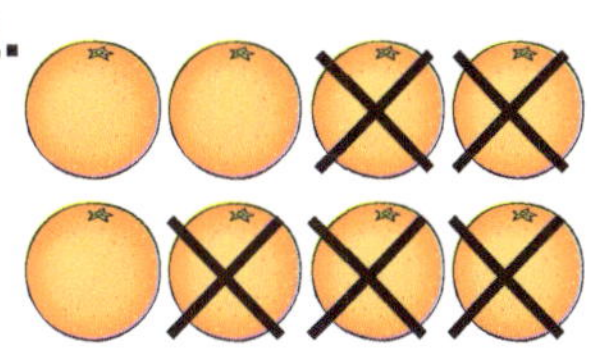

b. 

☐ - ☐ = ☐ ☐ - ☐ = ☐

2. a. 

= ☐ cents

b. 

= ☐ cents

3. a. 8 - 4 = ☐ b. 10 - 3 = ☐

A **noun** is a name we give to objects or things.
Add letters to these nouns.

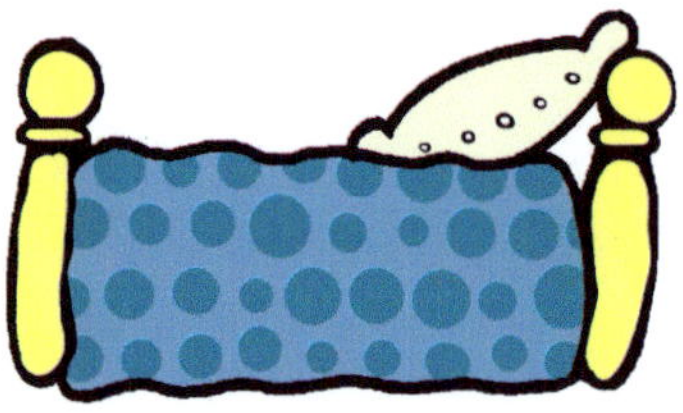

_ed

__oe

_us

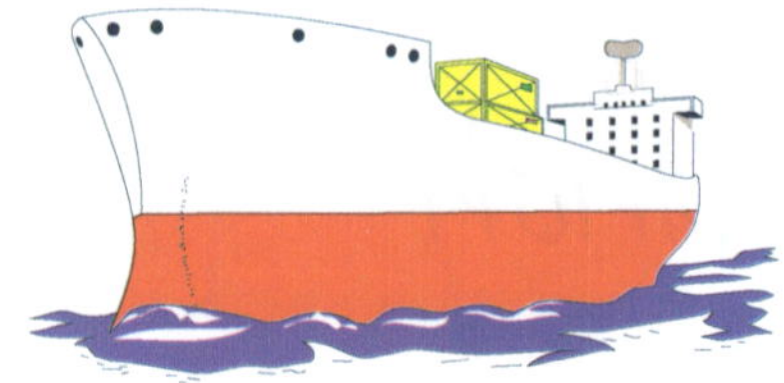

__ip

_alloon

_ish

_op

_irl

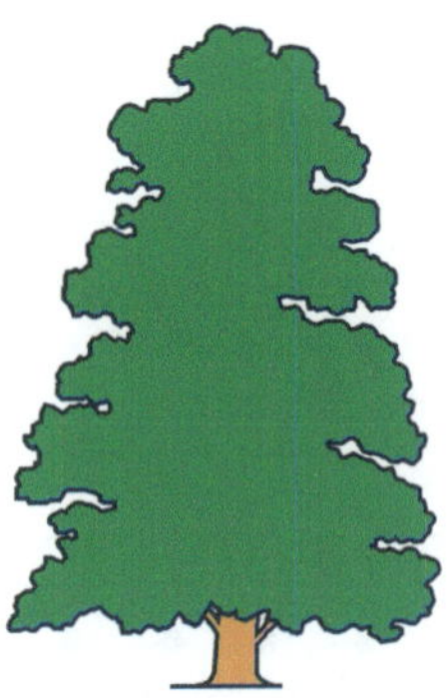

_ree

_at

_at

_ake

_ap

Writing

Add a noun from above to complete each sentence.

- Every morning dad goes to work by ___ ___ ___.
- Mum had to get a new ___ ___ ___.
- The little ___ ___ ___ ___ had a new dress.
- Our ___ ___ ___ likes to sit in the sun.
- My brother climed the big ___ ___ ___ ___.
- I lost a ___ ___ ___ ___ in the mud.

Rewrite each sentence adding a capital letter and a full stop.

- it will be my birthday next week

____

- mum was busy in the kitchen cooking dinner

____

- my family went on a picnic to the park

____

Months of the Year

Say the months of the year.

January February March April May June

July August September October November December

Complete these sentences.

- What month is it now? ____________________
- In what month do you have your birthday? ____________________
- What season is June, July, August? ____________________
- Write the months for Summer, then draw a summer picture.

____

____

____

Read the poem. Add a word to help complete it.

Summer days are lots of fun.
But do take care when in the sun.
Slip, slop, slap, is what to do.
To stop the sun from burning ________.

us
you
me
them

Writing

Write the words in the outlines, then match it to complete the slogan.

- on sun screen.
- on a shirt.
- on a hat.

Handwriting

Trace over the capital and lower case letters. Copy the sentence.

C C C C c c c c E E E E e e e e

Cats and elephants are cute.

Read the words. Trace over each letter, then copy and write each word.

words	trace	copy	write
slow	slow		
sleep	sleep		
slap	slap		
slide	slide		
slim	slim		

Write words from the list or poem that fit these outlines.

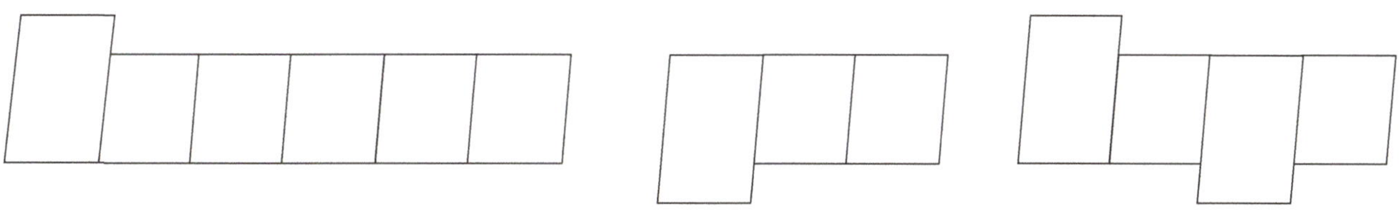

Money

Name these coins and note.

Data

Here is a graph about parked cars.

- How many red cars?
- How many blue cars?
- How many more red cars than yellow cars?
- How many cars in total?

Reading

Read the story, then complete the activities.

There are lots of stars in the sky at night. I can see them for most of the night from my bedroom window. At night when the moon shines brightly, the light comes in the window. It makes shadows on the wall.

At night, it is always quiet. Night is when we sleep, getting ready for tomorrow. I hope it's sunny in the morning.

Understanding

Draw a line to make sentences.

- Stars shine brightly at night
- Moonlight shining in the window

in the bedroom.

in the night sky.

makes wall shadows.

keeps me awake.

Interpreting

Colour the bubble that best fits the answers.

- Stars can be seen ◯ from my window. ◯ when it's sunny.
- Sleep helps us get ◯ always quiet ◯ ready for tomorrow.

Grammar

Nouns are also the names of people and places. These nouns all begin with a capital letter. Rewrite these names and places using a capital letter.

peta	josie	sydney	william
________	________	________	________
melbourne	caitlan	darcy	alley street
________	________	________	________

Spelling

Write the words.

th
- ____ree
- ____in
- ____ick
- ____roat
- ____under
- ____ing

Write these **th** words from the **th** family.

th
- ____e
- ____em
- ____ey
- ____an
- ____at
- ____ere
- ____is

Write words from the list or story that fit these frames.

Groups

1. Count how many in each row, then complete the sentence.

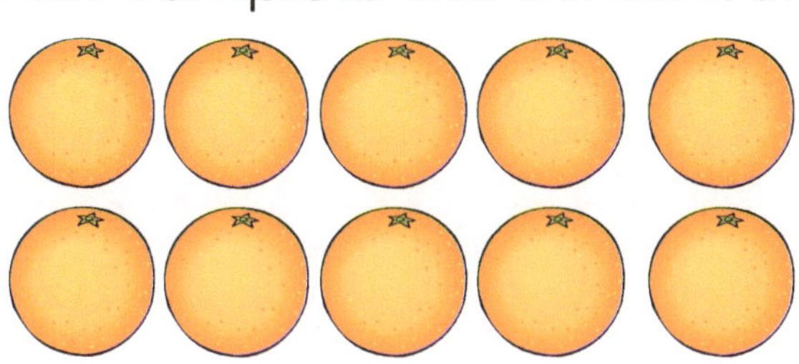

☐ rows of ☐ makes ☐

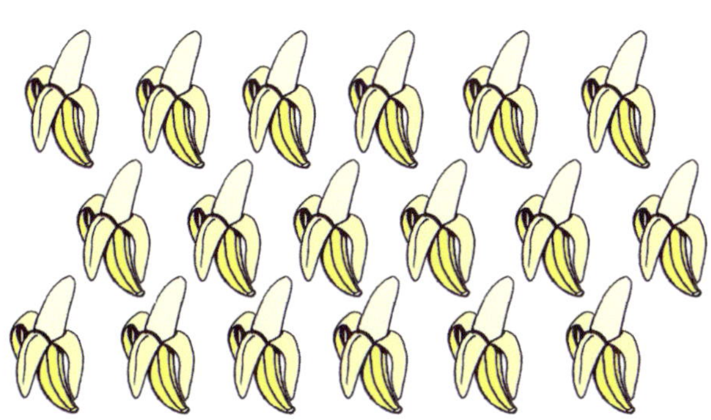

☐ rows of ☐ makes ☐

Time

1. What is the time?

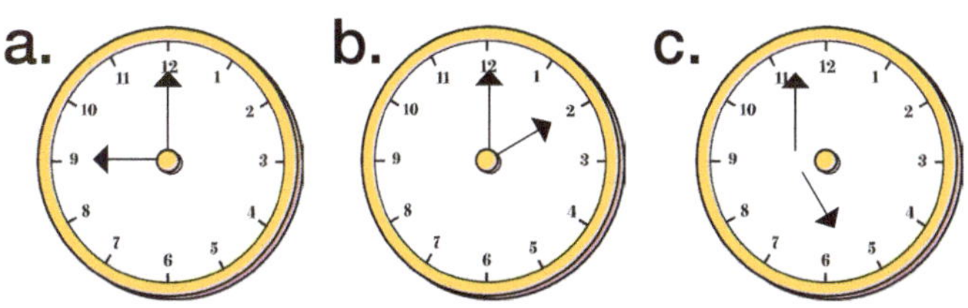

a. ____ o'clock b. ____ o'clock c. ____ o'clock

2. When the big hand points to the 6 it is half past the hour. The small hand is halfway between numbers. What time is it?

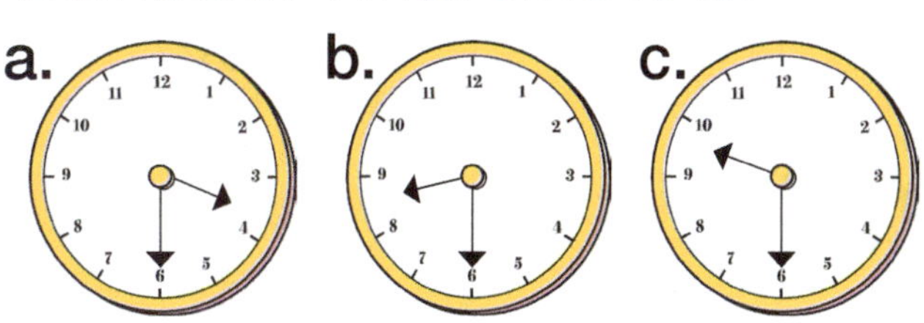

a. half past ☐ b. half past ☐ c. half past ☐

Read the story, then complete the activities.

Most people are scared of the eight legged, furry creatures, called spiders. Some are very dangerous but most only look scary. Spiders spin a silk web using their spinnerets. Webs are spun where spiders can catch their food. Flies and insects get stuck in the web. The spider then eats the fly or insect when it is hungry.

Understanding Draw a line to make sentences.

- Most spiders only look scary and
- Spiders spin a web to
- Spiders use their eight legs
- A spider web is made from

catch their food.

spider spin silk.

are not dangerous.

to spin a web.

Interpreting Colour the bubble that best fits the answers.

- Spiders like to eat ◯ flies and insects. ◯ people.
- Most people ◯ love spiders ◯ are scared of spiders.

Word Building

Add **sp** to make a list of words.

sp

- ___ ___ ider
- ___ ___ in
- ___ ___ ell
- ___ ___ ill
- ___ ___ ot
- ___ ___ ring
- ___ ___ inach

Response

Draw a spider, its web and an insect or a fly caught in the web.

Spelling

Write the words. Trace over the letters, then copy and write each word.

words	trace	copy	write
spider	spider		
spin	spin		
spot	spot		
spell	spell		
spring	spring		
sport	sport		

Write words from the list that best fit these outlines.

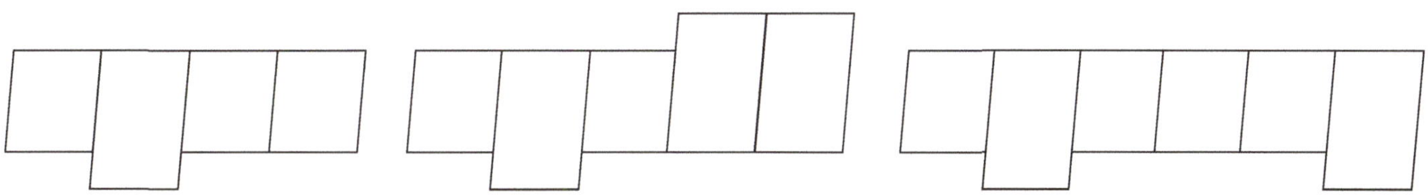

Length

Use a home key to measure the length of each object.

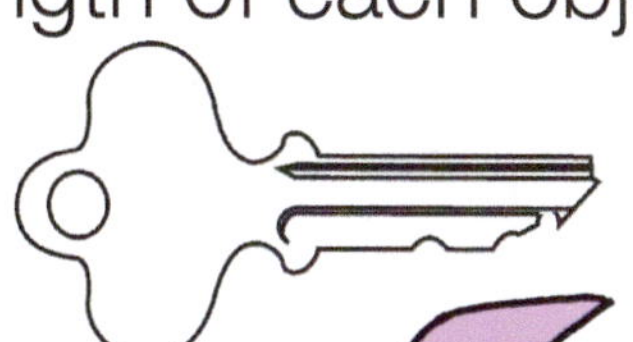

(a key like this)

☐ keys

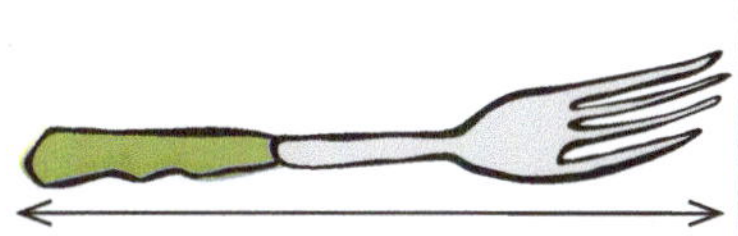

☐ keys

☐ keys

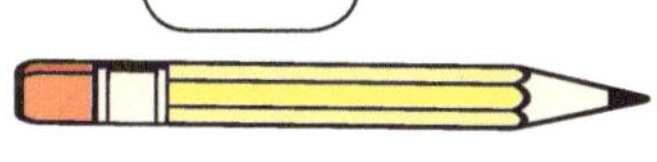

☐ keys

Patterns

Add the missing numbers to each pattern.

0	+	7	=	7
	+	6	=	7
	+	5	=	7
	+	4	=	7
	+	3	=	7
	+	2	=	7
	+	1	=	7
	+	0	=	7

0	+	8	=	8
	+	7	=	8
2	+		=	8
3	+	5	=	
	+	4	=	8
5	+		=	8
6	+		=	8
7	+	1	=	
8	+		=	8

Reading

Read the poem about a healthy body and food.

A strong healthy body and a strong healthy mind
Are both important to help us feel fine.
Eating good food won't make us fat.
This is important so we can do this or do that.
The five basic food groups should be eaten each day
So we can stay healthy to work and play.

Understanding

Draw a line to the best sentence ending.

- A healthy body has
- A strong healthy mind

a big fat belly.

strong bones and teeth.

allows us to do things.

helps us feel fine.

Interpretation

Colour the bubble that best fits an answer.

- There are ◯ five basic food groups ◯ all foods are good.
- A hamburger is: ◯ a healthy food ◯ not a healthy food.

Health and Society

Label each picture with a letter to show the food group to which it belongs.

M Meat/Fish/Poultry

F Fruit and Vegetables

D Dairy Food

B Bread and Cereal

O Oils and Fats

Read the words beginning with **'br'**.
Trace, copy and write each word.

word	trace	copy	write
bring	bring	______	______
brown	brown	______	______
bridge	bridge	______	______
bride	bride	______	______
brother	brother	______	______

Write words from the list that best fit these outlines.

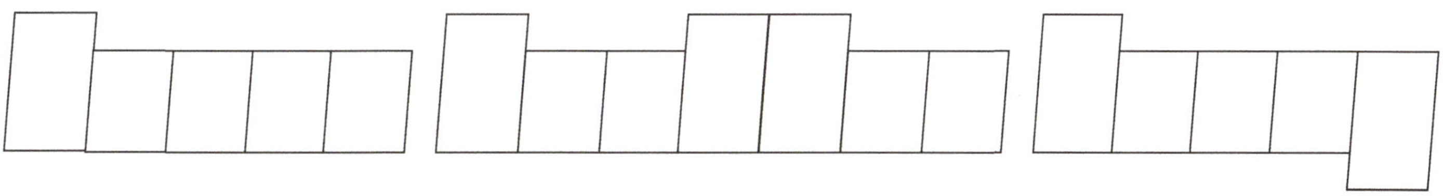

Mass

Order the mass of objects in each group lightest to heaviest. 1.2.3.

a. 

b. 

c. 

Counting by Fives

Count how many, then write the totals.

a.  = ☐ cents

b.  = ☐ dots

c. 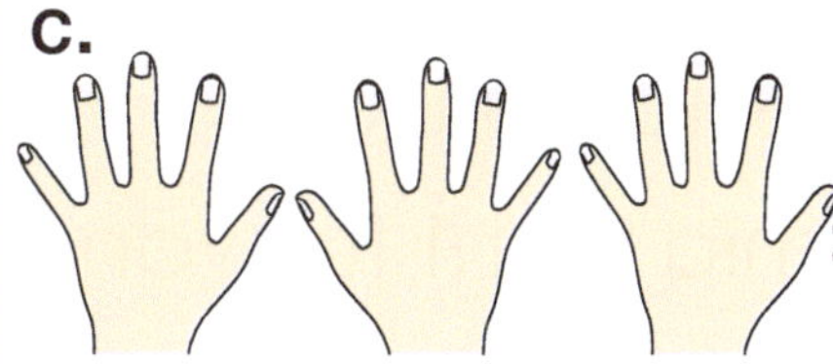 = ☐ fingers

d. 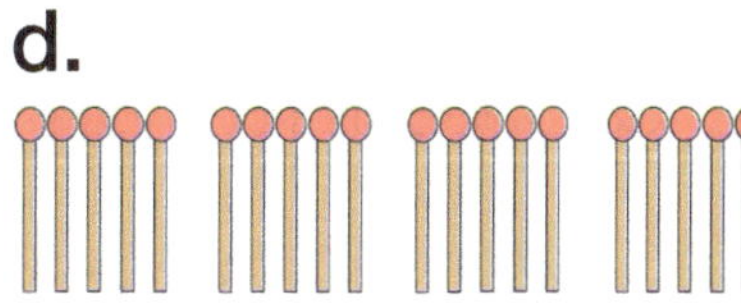 = ☐ matches

Read the poem. Discuss farms and the farmer.

A farmer must be fit and strong.
His working day is very long.
Milking cows or feeding the sheep
When does he find time to sleep.

Driving the tractor around and around
Planting seeds in the bone-dry ground.
Rain will bring him a bumper crop.
And for us, fresh food to get from the shop.

Understanding Colour the bubble that best fits an answer.

Farmers?

- ◯ are fit and strong
- ◯ are old
- ◯ sit on a tractor all day

Rain allows:

- ◯ us to use an umbrella
- ◯ plants to grow
- ◯ the garden to be watered

Response What am I?

- I am milked every day. I am a ______________ .
- I have four wheels and used on a farm. I am a ______________ .
- I help crops to drink and grow. I am ______________ .

Punctuation

Rewrite the sentences adding capital letters, full stops or question marks.

last week mia went to sydney to see her uncle jon

____

do you have a bike the same colour as james

____

Read the words beginning with **'st'**. Trace over the letters then copy and write each word.

word	trace	copy	write
strong	strong		
street	street		
string	string		
stop	stop		
stay	stay		
straw	straw		

Write words from the list that best fit these outlines.

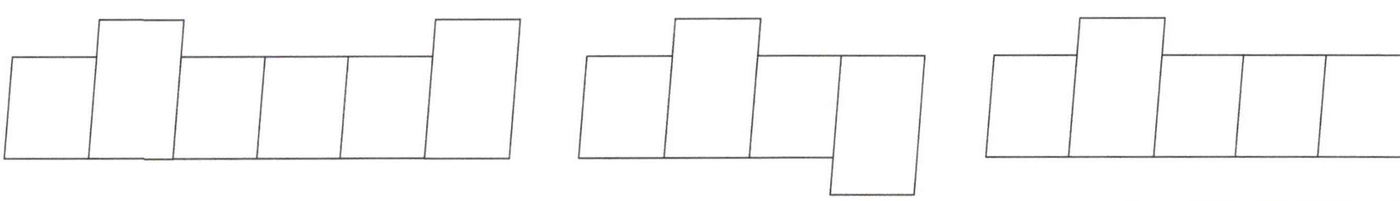

Symmetry

Draw the other half of each object.

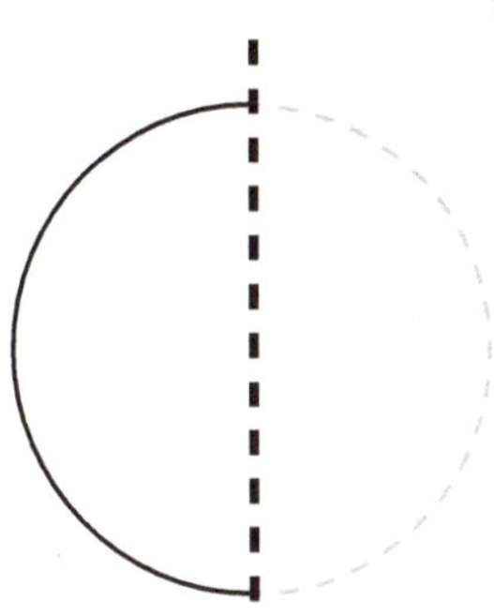

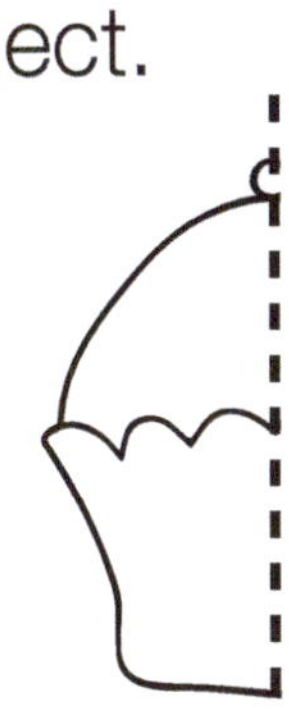

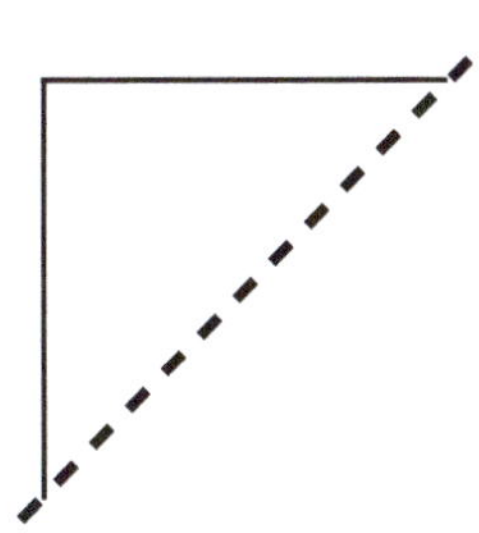

Patterns

Add the missing numbers in each pattern.

0	+	9	=	9
	+	8	=	9
	+	7	=	9
3	+	6	=	
	+	5	=	9
5	+	4	=	
6	+		=	9
7	+		=	9
	+	1	=	9
9	+	0	=	

0	+	10	=	10
	+	9	=	10
2	+		=	10
	+	7	=	10
4	+	6	=	
	+	5	=	10
6	+		=	10
7	+	3	=	
8	+		=	10
9	+	1	=	
10	+		=	10

Read the poem. Add the last rhyming word.

See the trees, hear the birds.
Today is lovely, mark my words.
Smell the flowers, taste the dew.
Will it rain? I wish I knew.
I will take my umbrella and my coat.
And all of you, please take a note.
When it rains, you will hear drops.
And enjoy the smell when it ________ .

Write words from the poem that rhyme with these words.

birds ________ dew ________ coat ________

My Senses

Match each word to the part of the body that senses it.

feel | smell | taste | look | hear

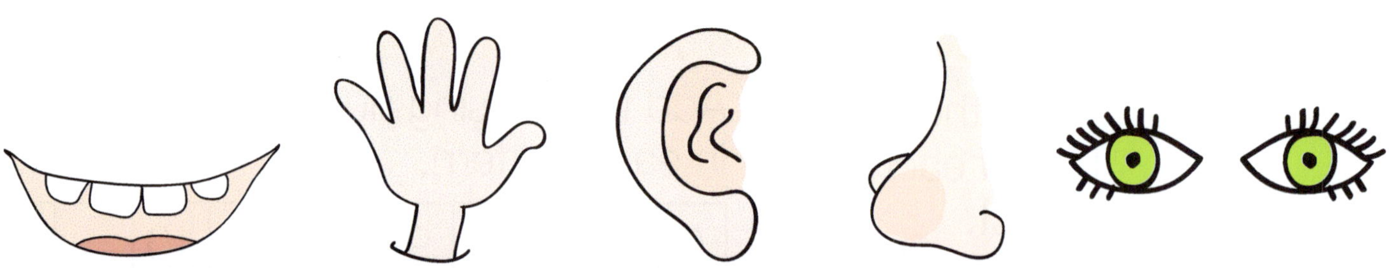

Handwriting

Trace over the capital and lower case letters.
Copy the sentence.

trace G G G G

trace g g g g

trace H H H H H

trace h h h h

Gardens grow when it rains.

copy

Read the words beginning with **'gr'**. Trace over the letters then copy and write each word.

word	trace	copy	write
grow	grow		
green	green		
grey	grey		
grub	grub		
grump	grump		
great	great		

Write words from the poem that best fit these outlines.

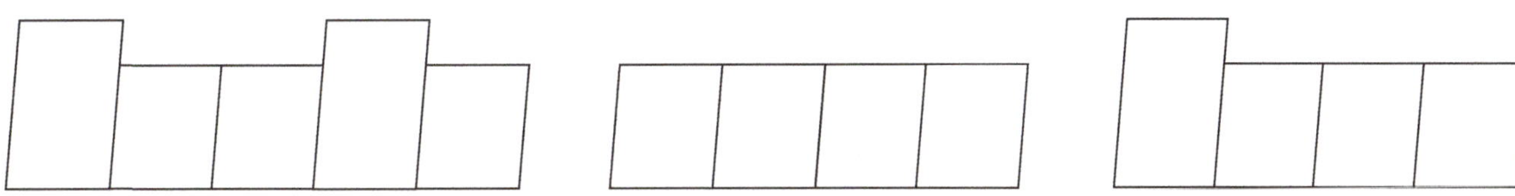

Capacity

Order 1-6 the counter that holds **the most to the least**.

a. 

b. 

c. 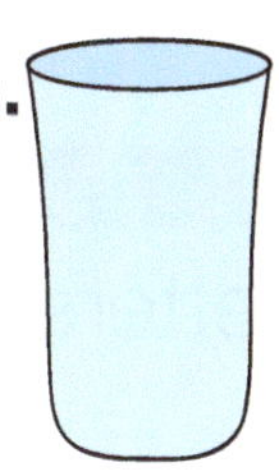

d. 

e. 

f. 

Counting by Tens

1. Count how many, then write the totals.

a. 

= ☐ cents

b. 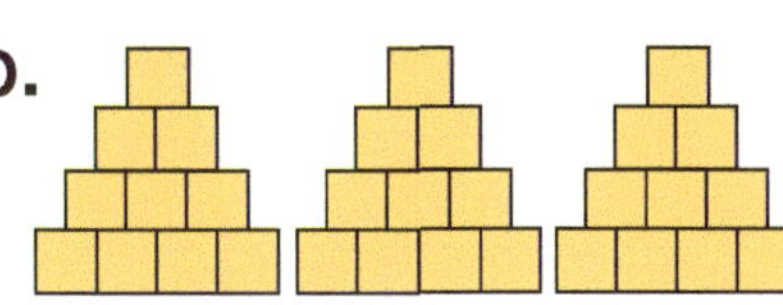 = ☐ blocks

c. 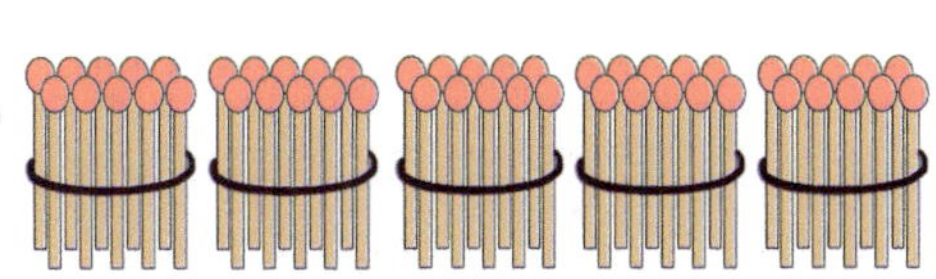 = ☐ matches

2. Fit in the missing tens.

10	20		40	50
60				100

Reading

Read the story about ants.

When Will and Mia woke up on Sunday they saw little ants marching around the top of the walls in the kitchen, lounge room, dining room and hallway. They rushed to find mum. She was still in bed.
"Mum, mum", cried Will. "You should see all the ants. There are hundreds of them!" Mum smiled and said "It must be going to rain. I will put some 'Antgo' around the kitchen. They will be gone by tomorrow."

Understanding

Draw a line to make sentences.

- Will and Mia saw
- Mum smiled because

the sun shining brightly.

little ants marching everywhere.

she knew what to do about ants.

it was going to rain.

Interpreting

Colour the bubble that fits the best answer.

- Ants come inside ◯ if it's going to rain. ◯ to march on walls.
- Mum was ◯ in the kitchen. ◯ still in bed.

Handwriting

Trace over the capital and lower case letters.

J J J J j j j j K K K K k k k k

M M M M m m m m N N N N n n n n

O O O O o o o o P P P P p p p p

Unit 18

Spelling

Look, cover, write, check each word.

word	write	check
when	______	☐
around	______	☐
rush	______	☐
find	______	☐
kitchen	______	☐
smile	______	☐

Word Building

Add **'all'** to build word families.

all

h___

b___

c___

t___

w___

sm___

st___

f___

Grammar

Remember nouns are names of things. People and place names are also nouns but need a capital letter. Add capital letters to these nouns.

__lana __unday __erth __arry

__arl __ia __pril __ohammed

Fractions

Colour a quarter of each shape or group.

a.

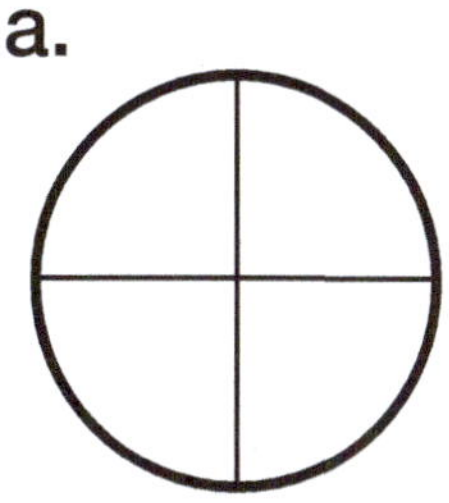

b.

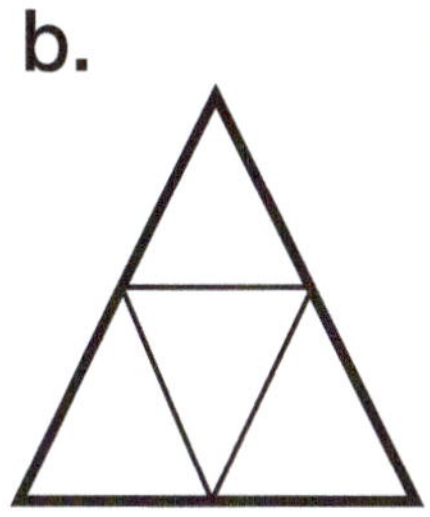

c.

d.

e.

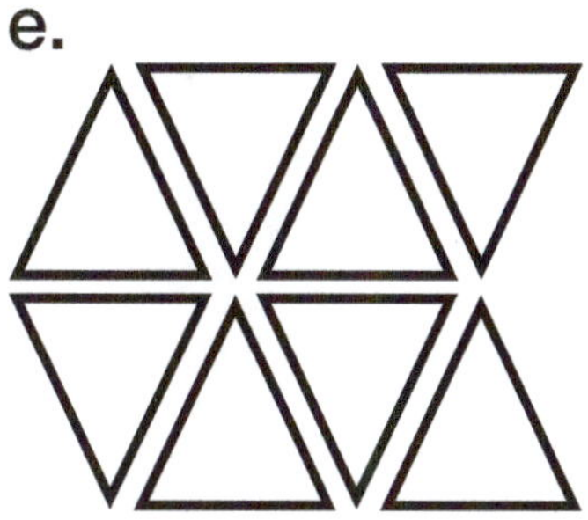

Money

Write how much in each piggy bank.

a.

☐ cents

b.

☐ cents

c. Add the value of these coins. Write the total.

$ ______

Read the poem. Discuss going to bed at night.

Go to sleep, say good night.
May you sleep all night long.
Go to sleep, say good night.
And I will sing you a night time song.
Go to sleep, say good night.
Close your eyes and hold them tight.
Go to sleep, say good night.
So the moon can shine soft light.

Write words from the poem that rhyme with these words.

long ________ night________ tight ________

Our Community

There are many people in our community who help us. Write words from the bank to label some of our helpers.

a.

____

b.

____

c.

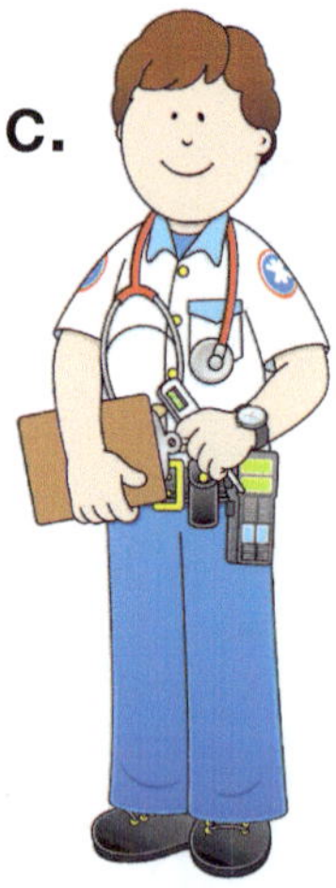

____

Word Bank

- Teacher
- Doctor
- Police officer
- Fireman
- Paramedic
- Dentist

d.

____

e.

____

f.

____

Unit 19

Spelling

Look, cover, write, check each word.

word	write	check
Monday	______________	☐
night	______________	☐
shine	______________	☐
doctor	______________	☐
teacher	______________	☐
cover	______________	☐

Word Building

Add **'ill'** to build word families.

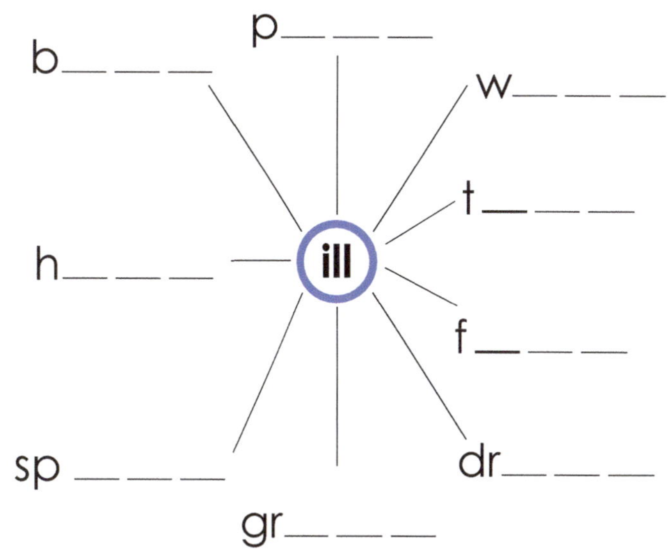

Write words from the poem or list that best fit these outlines.

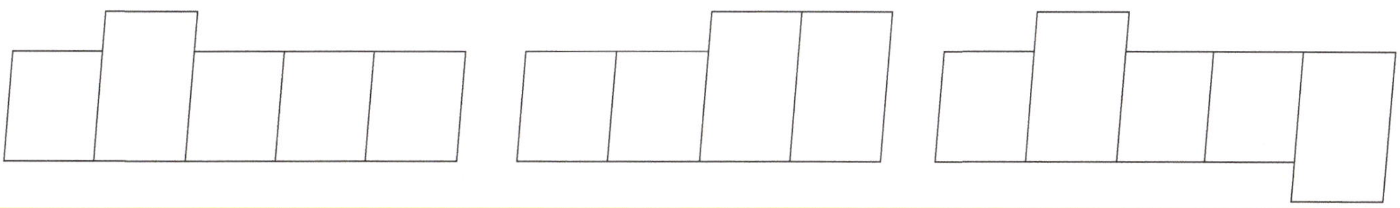

Subtraction

1. Colour the group, then write each number sentence.

a.

- - = ☐

b.

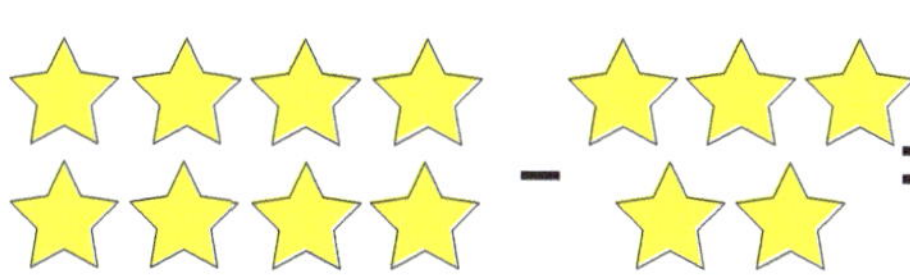

- - = ☐

2.

6	6	6	6	6	6
-1	-2	-3	-4	-5	-6
___	___	___	___	___	___

Take away Problems

1. Dad had 9 fish. Mum put 6 in the freezer. How many were left to cook?

☐ - ☐ = ☐ to cook

2. Kurt had $10. He spent $4. How much does he have left?

$☐ - $☐ = $☐ left

3. Bailey had 8 new footy cards. He gave Ali 3 cards. How many does Bailey have left?

☐ - ☐ = ☐ cards left

Reading

Read the poem. Discuss road safety.

"Click, clack front and back" is the road safety message we hear all the time. When we go shopping with mum in the car, she always checks that seat belts are done up. She checks that the baby seat is strapped on the back seat. Mum says you can never be too careful with seat belts because we are her pride and joy.

Understanding

Draw a line to make sentences.

- Click, clack front and back
- Mum checks our seat belts because

is a song we love to sing.

is a road safety message.

we can't do our belts up.

we are her pride and joy.

Interpreting

Colour the bubble that best fits the answer.

- Seat belts ◯ are in most cars. ◯ save lives.
- Babies are strapped in a seat ◯ in the front. ◯ in the back.

Handwriting

Trace over the capital and lower case letters.
Copy the sentence.

Q Q Q Q q q q R R R r r r S S S

s s s s U U U u u u V V V v v v

Gardens grow when it rains.

copy

Spelling

Look, cover, write, check each word.

word	write	check
click	______	☐
back	______	☐
black	______	☐
pack	______	☐
tack	______	☐
stack	______	☐

Word Building

Add **'ack'** to build word families.

ack

cr_ _ _
b_ _ _
t_ _ _
r_ _ _
p_ _ _
j_ _ _
tr_ _ _
bl_ _ _
sh_ _ _

Write words from the message about Road Safety or spelling list that best fit these outlines.

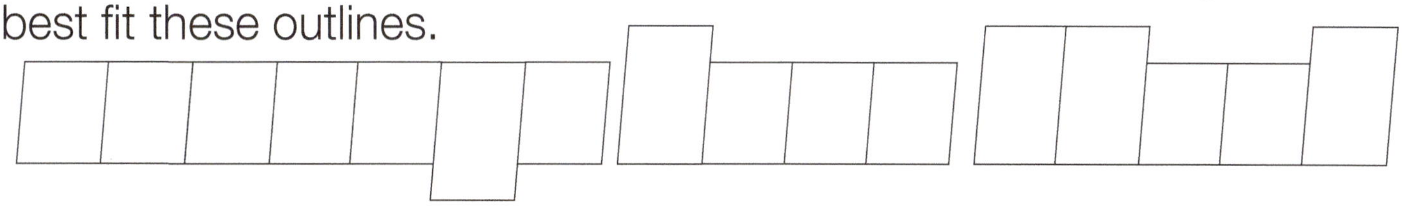

More or Less

1. Compare the numbers, colour the correct **more** or **less** card.

a. 7 is more / is less 6

b. 12 is more / is less 14

c. 22 is more / is less 53

d. 29 is more / is less 19

2. Write the number **2 more** than:

a. 19 ____ **b.** 42 ____ **c.** 13 ____

d. 11 ____ **e.** 28 ____ **f.** 40 ____

3. Write the number **2 less** than:

a. 16 ____ **b.** 11 ____ **c.** 25 ____

d. 29 ____ **e.** 30 ____ **f.** 33 ____

Addition

1. Count the groups, then write each number sentence.

a.

☐ + ☐ = ☐

b.

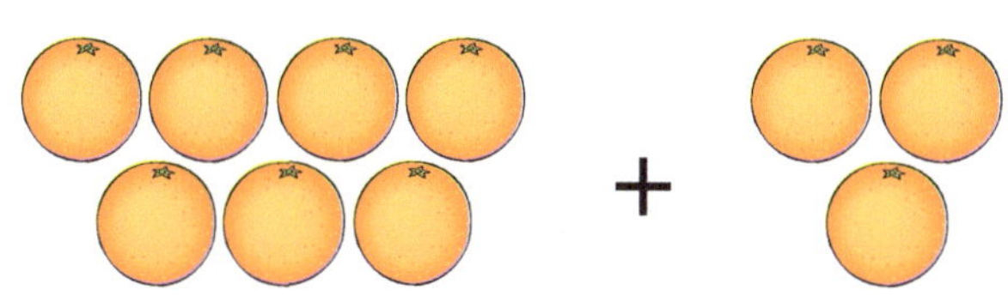

☐ + ☐ = ☐

c.

1	2	3	4	5	6
+2	+3	+4	+5	+2	+3
___	___	___	___	___	___

Reading Read the story about “Our Pets”, then complete the activities.

My big brother and I have three pets at home. A rabbit called Bugs, likes to eat leaves and carrots. Speedy, our turtle, likes to eat Bugs’ leaves too. Bugs doesn’t mind.

Last week dad came home with a baby kangaroo. We named her Penny. She drinks milk from a bottle.

Response Write a response to each question.

- How many pets do my brother and I have? ________________
- What are the names of the pets? ________________
- Why does Penny drink from a bottle? ________________

Grammar

Adjectives tell more about nouns. Select the best adjective from the list to describe each noun.

Adjectives
red
wet
sunny
little
sad
wet

________ day

__________ baby

____ afternoon

_____ elephant

_____ face

_____ car

Spelling

Look, cover, write, check each word.

word	write	check
rabbit	______	☐
turtle	______	☐
leaves	______	☐
from	______	☐
drink	______	☐
bottle	______	☐

Word Families

Add **'ell'** to build word families.

ell

t___ f___ y___ w___ sw___ sh___ s___ b___

Write words from the story or list that fit these outlines.

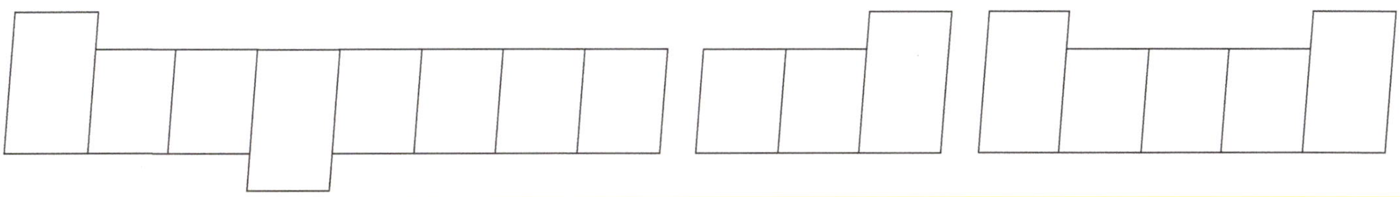

Time

1. Write the time shown on the "digital clock".

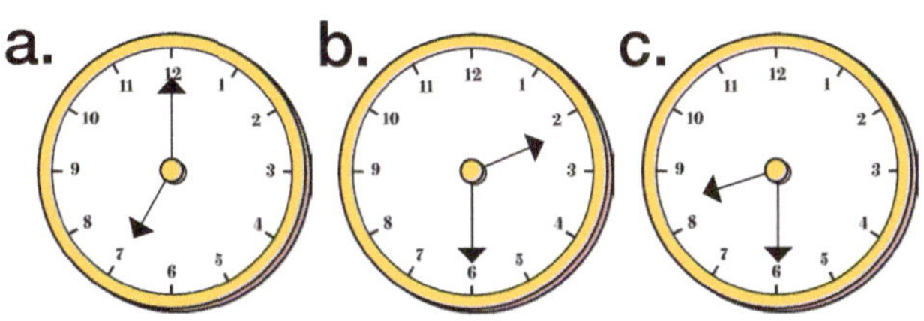

a. __ : __ b. __ : __ c. __ : __

2. Write the time on the digital clocks.

a. Half past one __ : __

b. Two o'clock __ : __

c. Half past nine __ : __

d. Half past ten __ : __

Addition

1. Count the groups, then write each number sentence.

a. 5 + 4 = ___

b. 7 + 1 = ___

c. 6 + 2 = ___

d. 3 + 7 = ___

e. 8 + 1 = ___

f. 5 + 3 = ___

g. 6 + 5 = ___

h. 4 + 8 = ___

2. Problem:

Fill in the number sentence.

Penny the hen laid 4 eggs and Henny 5 more. How many in total?

☐ + ☐ = ☐ eggs

Discuss these titles, then match them to the pictures.

Mr Mrs Miss Master Dr

Punctuation

Add capital letters, full stops or question marks to these sentences, then answer the questions adding punctuation.

- ☐hat is the name of your teacher ☐
  ☐y teacher's name is ____________ ○
- ☐n which month is your birthday ☐
  ☐y birthday is in ____________ ○

Handwriting

Trace over the capital and lower case letters.

W W W w w w Y Y Y y y y

X X X x x x x Z Z Z Z z z z z

copy copy copy

zoo x-ray you

Spelling

Look, cover, write, check each word.

word	write	check
letter		
mark		
name		
birthday		
teacher		
answer		

Word Building

Add **'ing'** to build word families.

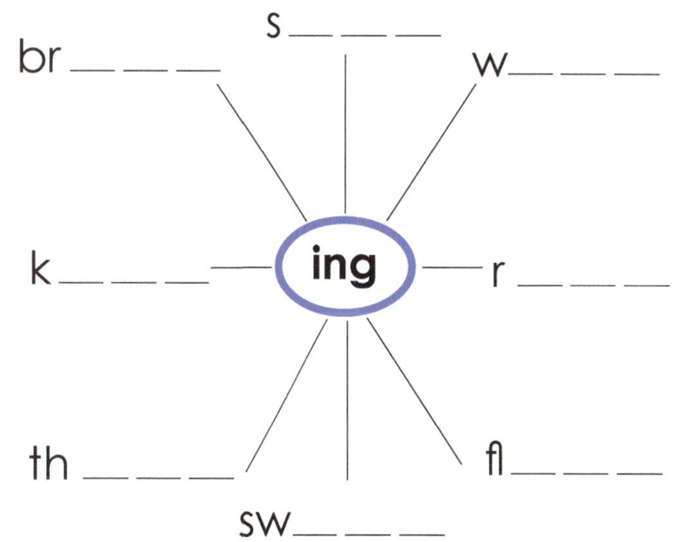

Write words from the story or list that fit these outlines.

Place Value

1. Write the number showing on each abacus.

a.

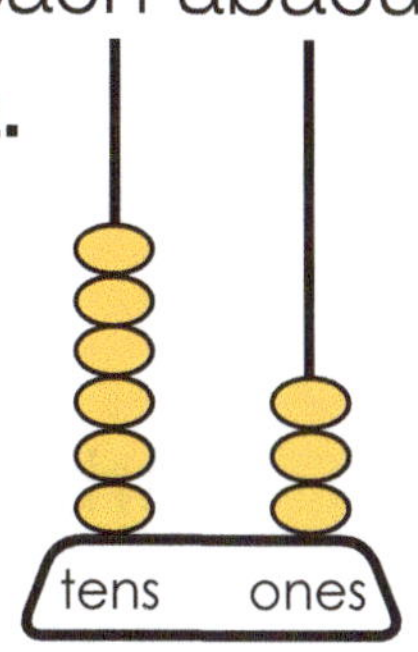

b.

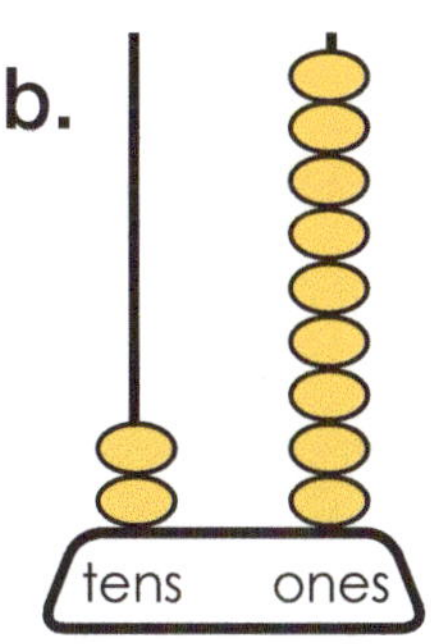

2. Draw beads on the abacus to show each number.

36

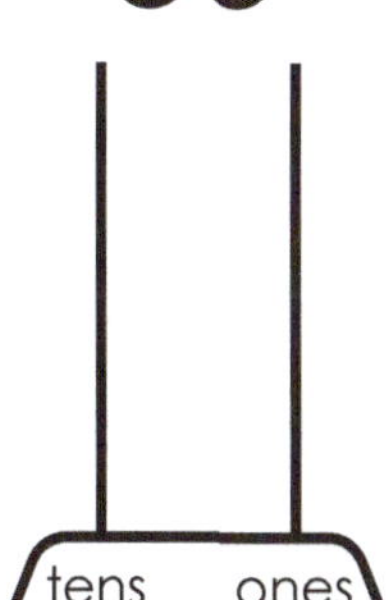

54

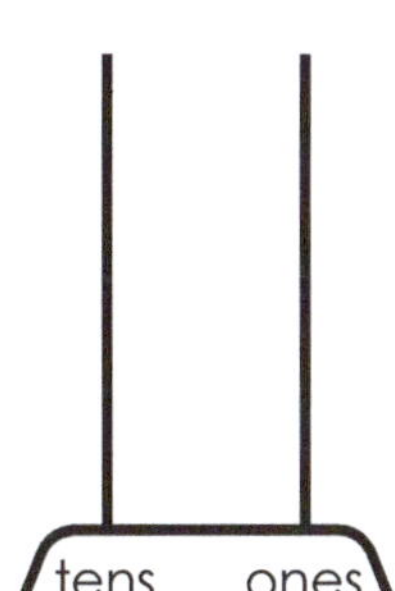

Chance

1. Colour the one most likely to happen by chance for each picture.

will happen
won't happen
might happen

will happen
won't happen
might happen

Reading

Unit 23

Read the story about the rain, then complete the activities.

When it rains the flowers, grass and trees grow. Rain helps the farmers grow their crops. It also fills our dams, so we have water to drink. Sometimes you can smell rain on the hot ground, after a storm. When I am in bed at night, I like to hear the rain "pitter-patter" on the roof.

Understanding

Draw a line to make sentences.

- Rain helps flowers, grass and trees
- You can smell rain after a storm

drink water.

all grow.

on the hot ground.

it pitter-patters.

Interpreting

Colour the bubble that best fits an answer.

- Rain helps ◯ fill our dams. ◯ fill our glasses.
- Rain is important ◯ in bed at night. ◯ to help crops grow.

Grammar

Verbs are action words. Select the best verb from the list that tells you what to do.

Verbs
sleep
run
eat
purr
sit
bark
read

______

______

______

______

______

______

______

Spelling

Look, cover, write, check each word.

word	write	check
flowers		
help		
smell		
drink		
roof		
storm		

Word Building

Add **'end'** to build word families.

end

l_ _ _

b_ _ _

m_ _ _

s_ _ _

sp_ _ _

fri_ _ _

bl_ _ _

Write words from the list or story that best fit these outlines.

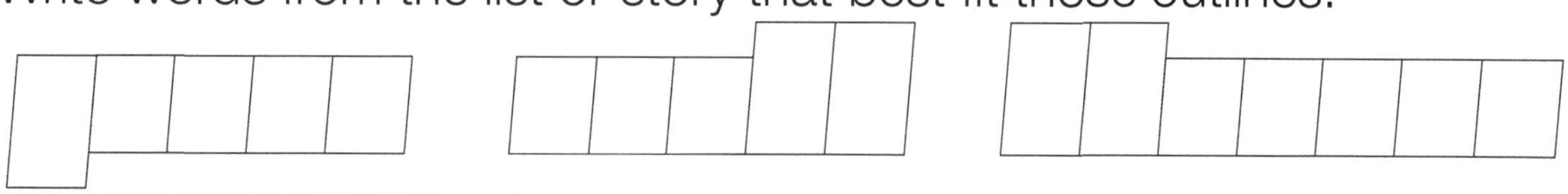

3D Objects

Colour the objects that will roll.

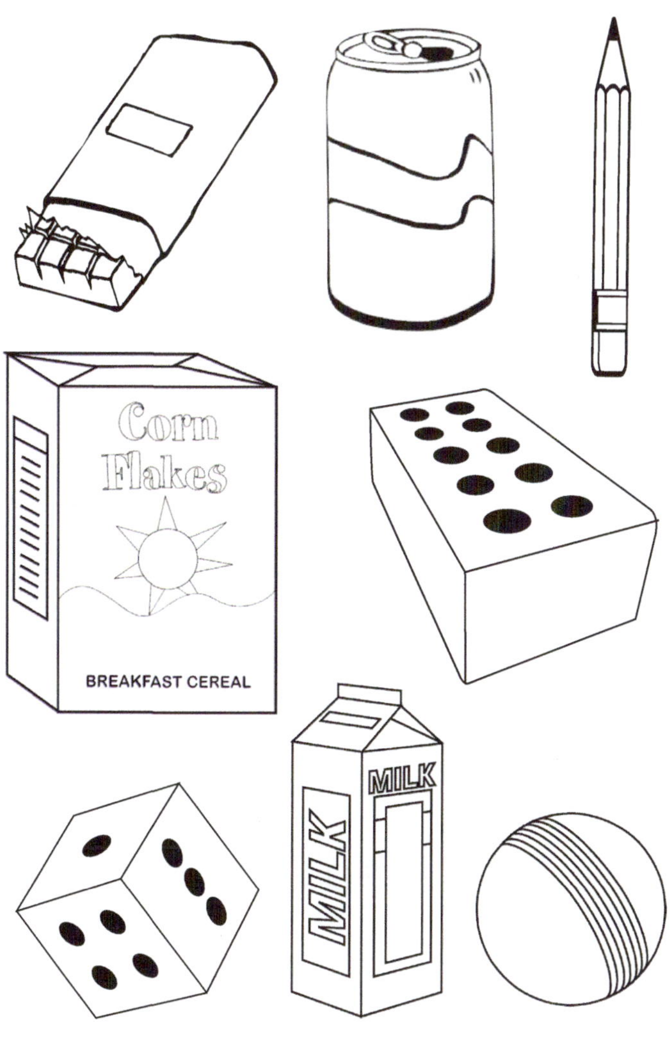

Equal groups

Colour the mittens to make pairs.

How many pairs of mittens?

Draw three equal groups of two.

Read the story about the circus.
Complete the activities.

"Roll up, roll up, come and see the circus. Watch the animals go 'round the big top. Hear the lions roar and see the monkeys play. High above the big top the flying trapeze will thrill the crowd."
"Hear the cheers and sounds of the circus. Come one, come all for a great night of fun for all the family."

Understanding

Draw a line to make sentences.

- The circus is held in
- The flying trapeze is

a big top.
in the park.
fun filled clowns.
high above the crowd.

Interpretation

Colour the bubble that best fits an answer.

- Roll up, roll up means
  - ◯ come and see.
  - ◯ watch the animals.
- Come one, come all
  - ◯ and see monkeys play.
  - ◯ for a great fun night.

Punctuation

Add capital letters, full stops or question marks to sentences.

a. ☐o you like biscuits☐
b. ☐an you skip☐
c. ☐t is cloudy today○
d. ☐ow old are you☐
e. ☐hen is your birthday☐

Sentences

Unjumble these sentences.
Put the verb first.

- the gate Close

____

- to the car Walk slowly

____

- at the red light Stop

____

Spelling

Look, cover, write, check each word.

word	write	check
clown		
crowd		
monkey		
watch		
circus		
great		

Word Building

Add **'and'** to build word families.

and

b_ _ _
l_ _ _
s_ _ _
h_ _ _
br_ _ _
st_ _ _
gr_ _ _
bl_ _ _

Write words from the list or story that best fit these outlines.

Numbers 1-100

1. Fill in the missing numbers.

1	2		4	5
	7	8		10
11			14	15
	17		19	

2. Write these as numbers.

a. seventy-eight

b. ninety-two

c. fifty-five

d. seventy-four

Money

1. Match each coin to its name.

twenty cents

one dollar

fifty cents

five cents

two dollars

ten cents

2. Add these coins and write the total.

=

Read the story "When I Grow Up", then complete the activities.

My name is Kurt and I am six. When I grow up I want to drive a fire engine. Firemen wear big yellow coats and hats. They wear their uniform every time they go to a fire. The uniforms must be hot. Dad said they wear their uniform so they don't get burnt. I want to be a fireman, when I grow up.

Understanding Draw a line to make sentences.

- Firemen wear
- Firemen wear their uniform

big yellow coats and hats.

thongs and T-shirts.

only when they drive the fire engine.

every time they go to a fire.

Interpretation Colour the bubble that best makes a sentence.

- Kurt ◯ wears a uniform. ◯ is six years old.
- Kurt's dad ◯ wants to be a fireman. ◯ explained why firemen wear their uniform.

Sentences

Unjumble these words and write sentences.

- tree Look that at ____________
- seat had Our belts bus ____________
- swim can Paris ____________
- can fast I run ____________
- is Saturday Tomorrow ____________

Unit 25

Spelling

Look, cover, write, check each word.

word	write	check
want		
drive		
yellow		
fire		
must		
wear		
fireman		

Sentences

Add a word from spelling list to make a sentence.

- The firemen went to the big .
- Dad likes to .
- Mum likes to her red dress.
- My favourite colour is .

Collating Data

1. Count each type of fruit. Colour a square on the graph for each type.

2. Which is the **most** fruit?

3. How many bananas?

4. How many apples?

5. Which fruits have the same amount?

6. How many more oranges than lemons?

7. How many pieces of fruit altogether?

Read the story about "Playing Cricket".

Last Saturday, my team played its first game of the season. We played the Wombats. Most of their team were seven and eight years old. They were a lot bigger than us.

When I went into bat, we had scored 18 runs. I scored 14 and we were all out for 76 runs.

When it was our turn to bowl the Wombat players kept getting out.

"Will, you bowled very well" said dad. The Wombats scored 52 runs.

"We won!" Big kids are not always that good!

Use words to complete each sentence.

seven	24 runs	Saturday	bat	players

a. We played cricket on ____________________ .

b. When I went into __________ we had scored eighteen runs.

c. The Wombats were __________ and eight years old.

d. The wombat _________ kept getting out.

e. We won by _____________ .

Punctuation

Add capital letters, full stops or question marks to these sentences.

a. ☐he ☐ombats were bigger than us○

b. ☐y how many runs did we beat the ☐ombats☐

c. ☐e sometimes play cricket on ☐unday afternoon○

d. ☐y name is ☐ill and ☐ like ☐aturday cricket○

Unit 26 Spelling

Look, cover, write, check each word.

word	write	check
play		
seven		
most		
turn		
always		
were		
team		

Word Building

Add **'y'** to build word families.

y

m___
cr___
fr___
sl___
sp___
dr___
fl___
sk___
b___
wh___

Write words from the list or story that best fit these outlines.

Subtraction

1.

a. $\begin{array}{r} 8 \\ -2 \\ \hline \end{array}$

b. $\begin{array}{r} 9 \\ -4 \\ \hline \end{array}$

c. $\begin{array}{r} 10 \\ -6 \\ \hline \end{array}$

d. $\begin{array}{r} 7 \\ -5 \\ \hline \end{array}$

2. Kate had 12 balloons. She gave 5 to her brother. How many does she have left.

☐ - ☐ = ☐ balloons left

3. Take the numbers down the side from the top numbers.

-	7	9	10	8	6
4					
2					

Skip Counting

1. Count on by 2s. Write the numbers.

24							38

2. Count by 10 to add the coins.

How much? ☐ cents

3. Skip count by 5s

What is the total number of dots and the last number? ☐

Read the story "Getting Ready".

My family start getting ready for holidays in November. Dad gets out all the camping gear. Mum gets all the tinned food ready. William gets his bike all cleaned and Jessie, my little sister, gets out all her holiday clothes and lays them on the spare bed in her room. I laugh, then go and watch television. It is only November. We have weeks before it's after Christmas.

Use words to complete each sentence.

clothes	camping	November	Jessie	watch

a. Jessie lays her holiday ______________ on the spare bed.

b. Dad starts to organise all the ______________ gear.

c. The family starts getting ready for holidays in ______________ .

d. I like to go and ___________ television.

e. My little sister's name is ______________.

Understanding

Colour the bubble that best makes a sentence.

a. Jessica is
- ◯ younger
- ◯ older

b. My brother's name is
- ◯ William
- ◯ Kurt

c. On holidays we all go
- ◯ like to watch television
- ◯ camping

d. Who gets the bike all clean?
- ◯ Jessie
- ◯ William

e. What month do we go camping?
- ◯ November
- ◯ December

f. How many in our family?
- ◯ 4
- ◯ 5

Unit 27

Spelling

Look, cover, write, check each word.

word	write	check
holidays		
clean		
ready		
start		
cloth		
watch		

Word Families

Add **'br'** to build word families.

br

__ __ ing

__ __ ick

__ __ anch

__ __ ead

__ __ ide

__ __ other

__ __ ush

__ __ oom

Write words from the list or story that best fit these outlines.

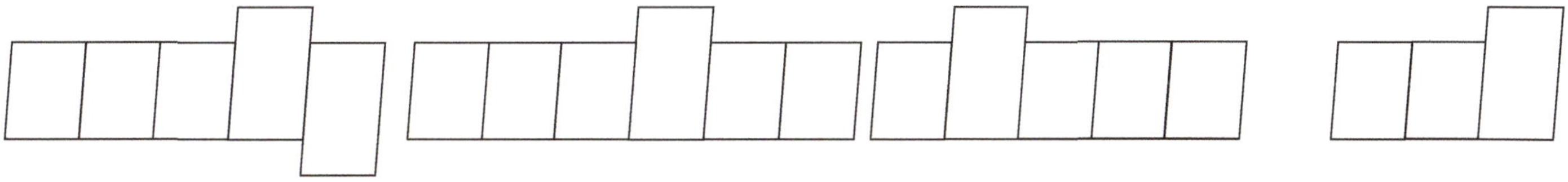

2D shapes

Trace over the shapes. Match each shape to its name. Colour them.

a. 

b. 

c. 

d. 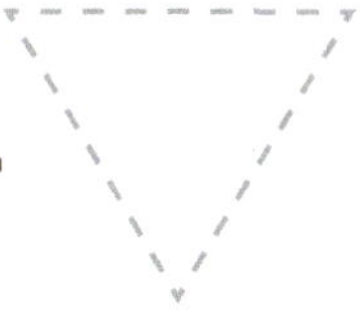

e.

pentagon

circle

square

octagon

triangle

Months of the Year

1. Say the months of the year.

January February March

April May June

July August September

October November December

2. Colour the month it is now.

3. Which is the **6th** month of the year?

____

4. How many days in **June**? ☐

5. How many days in **July**? ☐

Read the story, then complete the activities.

Next week is the start of December. School will end soon and I will be sad. I like my teacher, Mrs Jones. She is a good teacher. Rosie Hampton, who I have sat near all year, is my best friend. Paris, Eva and Mia are my friends too. We played in the same netball team.

Next year I will be in Year 2. I hope I get Mrs Freeman as my teacher. She is very friendly. I hope Rosie and I can sit together next year too.

Understanding

Use words to complete sentences.

Mrs Freeman	netball	Rosie	November	school

a. Paris, Eva, Mia and I all played ______________ together.

b. My best friend is ______________ Hampton.

c. What month is it now in the story? ______________

d. Next year I hope my teacher will be ______________.

e. I will be sad because ______________ will end.

Handwriting

Copy the sentences.

I like to feed my pet fish.

Spelling

Look, cover, write, check each word.

word	write	check
week	____________	☐
teacher	____________	☐
friend	____________	☐
together	____________	☐
hope	____________	☐
December	____________	☐
same	____________	☐

Grammar

Plural means more than one. We can add **'s'** to make nouns plural.
dog (s)

cat___ table___ day___

night___ month___

week___ tree___ boy___

bird___ book___ team___

girl___ mother___

Write words from the list that best fit these outlines.

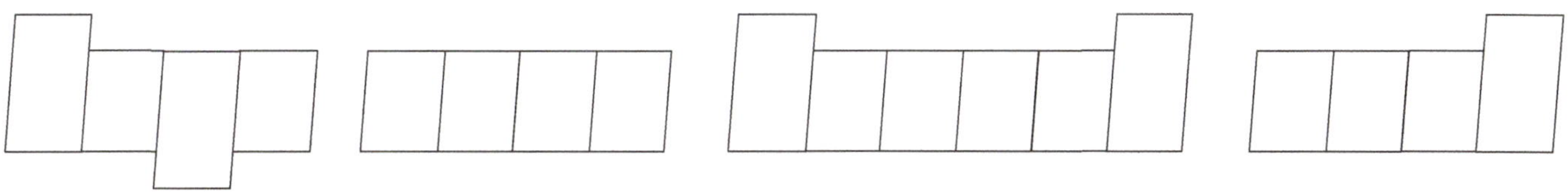

Capacity

Order 1-6, from those holding most to those holding least.

a.

☐

b.

☐

c.

☐

d.

☐

e.

☐

f.

☐

Chance

Colour the chance of the event happening.

will happen
won't happen
might happen

will happen
won't happen
might happen

will happen
won't happen
might happen

Pronouns are used in place of nouns. e.g. he.
Use pronoun in each sentence.

he she they them it we you her him me

a. Paris and Emma saw a horse. ________ saw a horse.

b. Jose jumped in the car. ____ was going to Sydney.

c. Will and Harry wore their uniform. Mum said, look at ________.

d. I saw a big spider. You should have seen ____ .

e. Amy came to school by car. ______ mother drove the car.

f. Peta, Li and I won a prize. ____ won three chocolates.

g. My sister is older than ____. ______ is in Year 5.

h. I saw ______ at the movies last Saturday.

i. Look at ______ standing over there, said Mrs Freeman.

Group

1. Label each group.

a.

☐ groups of ☐ = ☐

b.

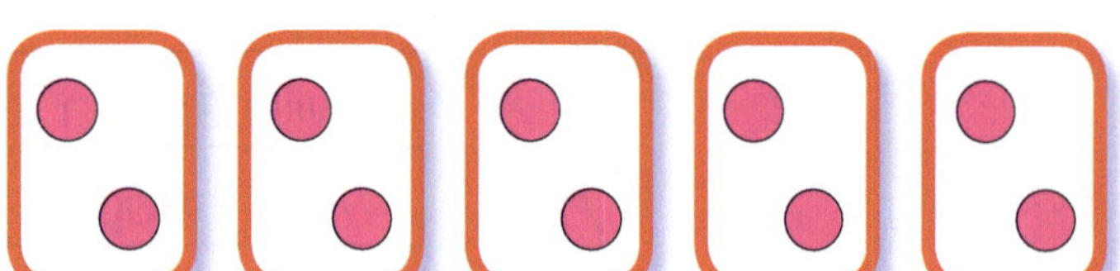

☐ groups of ☐ = ☐

2. Use colour to make 3 equal groups.

Seasons

1. Write the months of summer.

____

____

____

2. Draw a summer picture.

Unit 30 — Money

Match each note to its name.

a. 

b. 

c. 

| five dollars | ten dollars | twenty dollars | fifty dollars | one hundred dollars |

d. 

e. 

Subtraction

Fill in the missing number.

a.  − ☐ = 7

b.  − ☐ = 4

c.  − ☐ = 3

Time

1. What time is it?

a. 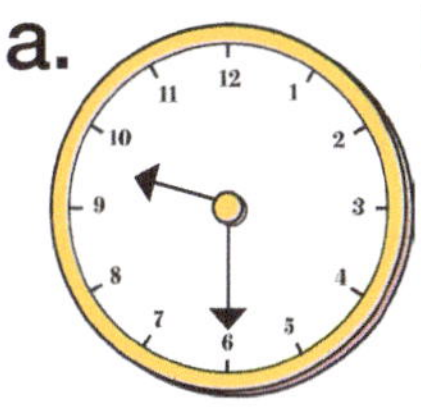

☐ : ☐

b. 

☐ : ☐

c. 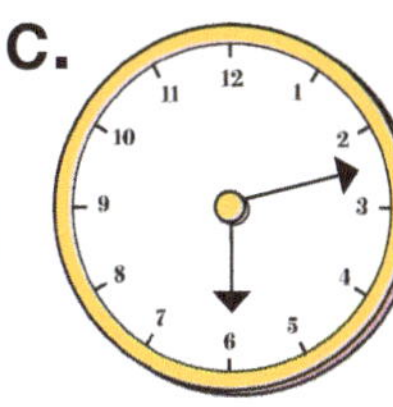

☐ : ☐

2. Write these times in digital form.

a. half past six ☐ : ☐

b. five o'clock ☐ : ☐

c. half past eleven ☐ : ☐

d. seven o'clock ☐ : ☐

Sentences

Colours can be adjectives. Choose a colour adjective to complete sentences.

| red | blue | black | pink | green |

a. The grass was a healthy ______________ in colour.

b. The sky is ______________ today.

c. Dad bought a new ______________ car.

d. The rose was a pretty soft ______________.

e. The big ______________ bus came around the corner.

Answers

Unit 1	pool. chops. / shops. swim. / Friday cat bat hat mat rat / today, mum, she, swim / My ⊙ On Friday ⊙ / **a.** 2,3 **b.** 1,4 **c.** 5,0 **d.** 6,3 / Monday, Thursday, Saturday
Unit 2	six shop / mix six six / bet let wet jet get set pet vet net met / cake mum net / shop girl dad cake / dad cake girl / 6+3+5=14 4+7+6=17 7+4+7=18 / 
Unit 3	Parent / 12 months. / top mop stop shop / baby boy cot balloon fish / Parent / fish boy school day / school fish boy / **a.** 7 o'clock **b.** 3 o'clock **c.** 10 o'clock / **a.- e., b.- f., c.- d., a.** elephant **b.** dice / **d. f. c. b. a. e.**
Unit 4	Yes, 3, yes, one. / wool, boy, little, one, sheep, three, yes, down / pig, big, yes gate / little big gate / **a.** bucket **b.** sulo bin **c.** bath / 10-4=6 8-3=5 12-5=7
Unit 5	rain, wind, sun, snow / spring / Parent - answers will vary. / sit, hit, lit, mit, bit, fit, kit, pit, wit / flowers rain clouds / wind rain always spring flowers / rain winter always / **a.** 30 **b.** 40 **c.** 20 **d.** 60 / sixty 60, thirty 30, fourty 40, twenty 20, ninety 90, one hundred 100, seventy 70, ten 10, fifty 50, eighty 80
Unit 6	We have a dog, cat and turtle at home. Molly is the name of our cat. Speedy is a turtle that likes to eat leaves. Scruffy tries to eat the cat food. / every afternoon turtle / map tap cap pan lap fan / food turtle letuce fluffy / afternoon tail every each like / sister every each or tail / one dollar two dollars fifty cents twenty cents five cents ten cents / apples 5, bananas 6, oranges 4, pears 4, bananas / pears and oranges / 19
Unit 7	some chickens are on a chair. Henny Penny is my pet chicken. Mum cooks chicken in a pot. There are lots of chickens everywhere. / chirp a lot in a pot. / chicken children chips chair church cheese / Spelling - Parent check / some ground chair / circle square triangle rectangle hexagon pentagon /  / 
Unit 8	My old shoes had worn out. Mum took me to buy shoes. Shelley needed shoes too. The shoe man said my feet had grown. / grow every year a good memory / shoe ship shovel shirt / Spelling - Parent check. / shoe shop shirt / sphere pyramid cube cylinder cone prism / **a. b. d.**
Unit 9	Parent / Eating good food helps keep us healthy. Fun foods I like to eat are biscuits and cakes. The food I like best is a cream bun. / Parent! / food cake bread / **1.a.**53 **b.**49 **c.**28 **2a.**85 **b.**74 **1.**5+3=8, 6+5=11 **2a.**5+8=13 **b.**5+4=9
Unit 10	First mum and Will washed the floors. Will was happy to make lunch because he liked food. Will was grounded last Sunday afternoon. / he was grounded he will do more cleaning. / Will was grounded last Sunday afternoon. On Saturday Will and Paris went to Sydney. / Parent check spelling / lunch help afternoon / 5, 9, 3, 1, 7, 11 / **1.a.** 8-5=3 **b.** 9-2=7 / **2a.** 10 cents **b.** 30 cents **c.** 4 **d.** 7

Answers

Unit 11	bed shoe bus ship balloon fish mop girl tree hat cat cake cap / bus hat girl cat tree shoe / It will be my birthday next week. Mum was busy in the kitchen cooking dinner. My family went for a picnic to the park. / Parent / Parent / Winter / December, January, February / Parent.
Unit 12	you / slop on sunscreen, slip on a shirt, slap on a hat. / Parent check spelling / summer you days / 5 cents, 50 cents, one dollar, ten cents, 20 cents, two dollars, five dollars / 5 red, 4 blue, 2 more red, 15 cars
Unit 13	in the night sky / makes wall shadows / from my window, ready for tomorrow. Peta Josie Sydney William Melbourne Caitlan Darcy Alley Street / three thin thick throat thunder thing / the them they than that there this / three thing thick / 2 rows of 5 =10, 3 rows of 6 =18 **1.a.** 9 o'clock **b.** 2 o'clock **c.** 5 o'clock / **2.a.** 3 **b.** 8 **c.** 9
Unit 14	...are not dangerous., ...catch their food., ...to spin a web., ...spider spin silk (gossamer). / flies and insects. are scared of spiders. / spider spin spell spill spot spring spinach / Spelling - parents to check / spin spell spring / scissors 3-5, fork 4-5, shoe 5-6, pencil 3 / 1,2,3,4,5,6,7 / 1,6,8,4,3,2,8,0.
Unit 15	...strong bones and and teeth., ...helps us feel fine. / five basic food groups. not a healthy food./ carrot F, cheese D, milk D, apple F, bread B, fish M, cake B, chips O / Parent - check spelling / brown, brother, bring / **a.** letuce, orange, pumpkin, **b.** man, fridge, elephant, **c.** paddle, racket, cricket bat / **a.** 20 cents **b.** 20 dots **c.** 15 fingers **d.** 20 matches.
Unit 16	are fit and strong. plants to grow. / cow, tractor, rain (water) / Last week Mia went to Sydney to see her unkle Jon. Do you have a bike the same colour as James? / Parent - check spelling / street stop straw / / 1,2,9,4,9,3,2,8,9 / 1,8,3,10,5,4,10,2,10,0.
Unit 17	stops. / words, knew, note / taste feel hear smell look / Parent - check spelling / birds rain hear / **e.** bucket **f.** soft drink **a.** fizzy drink **c.** glass **b.** wine glass **d.** egg cup. / **a.** 40 cents **b.** 30 blocks **c.** 50 matches **2.** 30, 70, 80, 90
Unit 18	...little ants marching everywhere., it was going to rain. / if it is going to rain., still in bed. / Parent - check spelling / ball tall small fall stall wall call hall / Alana Sunday Perth Harry Carl Mia April Mohammed / **a.** **b.** **c.** **d.** **e.** / **a.** 35 cents **b.** 65c, $1.75
Unit 19	song tight light / **a.** Fireman **b.** Police officer **c.** Paramedic **d.** Doctor **e.** Dentist **f.** Teacher / Parent - check spelling / bill hill spill grill drill fill till will pill / shine will sleep / **a.** 4-2=2 **b.** 8-5=3 **2.** 5, 4, 3, 2, 1, 0 **1.** 9-6=3 fish to cook **2.** $10 - $4 = $6 left **3.** 8 - 3 = 5 cards left
Unit 20	...is a road safety message., ...we are her pride and joy. / save lives. in the back. / Parent - check spelling / back pack track shack black Jack rack tack crack **1a.** more **b.** less **c.** less **d.** more **2a.** 21 **b.** 44 **c.** 15 **d.** 13 **e.** 30 **f.** 42 **3a.** 14 **b.** 9 **c.** 23 **d.** 27 **e.** 28 **f.** 31 / **a.** 5+3=8 **b.** 7+3=10 **c.** 3,5,7,9,7,9

Answers

Unit 21	Three / Bugs, Speedy, Penny / Because Penny is a baby. **/** sunnu day, wet afternoon, little baby, big elephant, sad face, red car. **/** Parent **/** bell sell shell swell well yell fell tell **/** kangaroo eat drink **/ 1.a.**7:00 **b.** 2:30 **c.** 8:30 **2a.** 1:30 **b.** 2:00 **c.** 9:30 **d.** 10:30 **/ 1a.** 9 **b.** 8 **c.** 8 **d.** 10 **e.** 9 **f.** 8 **g.** 11 **h.** 12 **/** 4+5=9 eggs
Unit 22	Miss (girl) Master (boy) Mrs (lady) Dr (doctor) Mr (man) **/** W? , M. , I?, M. **/** Spelling - parent check **/** bring king thing swing fling ring wing sing **/** name month letter **/ 1.a.** 63 **b.** 29 **2.a.** 36 **b.** 54 **1. a.** won't happen **b.** will happen
Unit 23	...all grow., ...on the hot ground. **/** fill our dams. to help crops grow.**/** purr, sleep, eat, sit, bark, run, read **/** Parent check **/** bend send friend blend spend mend lend **/** grass smell flowers **/** can pencil ball(dice) **/** 6 pairs **/** Parent
Unit 24	...a big top., ...high above the crowd. come and see. for a great fun night. **/ a.** D? , **b.** C? , **c.** I. , **d.** H? **e.** W? **/** Close the gate. Walk slowly to the car. Stop at the red light. **/** Spelling - parent check **/** band hand stand grand bland brand sand land **/** monkey crowd clowns cheers **/ 1.** 3, 6, 9, 12, 13, 16, 18, 20 **2.a.** 78 **b.** 92 **c.** 55 **d.** 74 **1.** ten cents one dollar 2 dollars 5 cents twenty cents 50 cents **2.** 65 cents
Unit 25	...big yellow coats and hats., ...every time they go to a fire. **/** is six years old explained why firemen wear their uniform (protective gear). **/** Look at that tree. Our bus had seat belts. Paris can swim. I can run fast. Tomorrow is Saturday. **/** Spelling - parent check **/** fire drive wear yellow. **/** 4 squares 3 squares 2 squares 5 squares 2 squares. **2.** oranges **3.** 2 **4.** 4 **5.** bananas, lemons **6.** 3 more **7.** 16 pieces.
Unit 26	**a.** Saturday **b.** bat **c.** seven **d.** players **e.** 24 runs **/ a.** TW. **b.** BW? **c.** WS. , **d.** MWBJIS. **/** Spelling - parent check **/** why by cry by sky fly dry spy sly fry cry my **/** last play always **1.a.** 6 **b.** 5 **c.** 4 **d.** 2 **2.** 12-5=7 balloons left **3.** 3,5,6,4,2/5,7,8,6,4 **1.** 26,28,30,32,34,36 **2.** 40 cents **3.** 25
Unit 27	**a.** clothes **b.** camping **c.** November **d.** watch **e.** Jessie **/ a.** younger **b.** William **c.** camping **d.** William **e.** December **f.** 4 **/** Parent check! **/** broom brush brother bride bread branch brick bring **/** ready sister clean out **/ a.** square **b.** pentagon **c.** circle **d.** triangle **e.** octagon **1. / 2.** Parent **3.** June **4.** 30 **5.** 31
Unit 28	**a.** netball **b.** Rosie Hampton **c.** November **d.** Mrs Freeman **e.** school **/** Spelling - parent check **/** cats tables days nights months weeks trees boys birds books teams girls mothers **/** hope same friend week **/ e.**1 **b.** 2 **f.** 3 **d.** 4 **a.** 5 **c.** 6 **a.** won't happen **b.** will happen **c.** might happen
Unit 29	**a.** They **b.** He **c.** them **d.** it **e.** Her **f.** We **g.** me. She **h.** you **i.** him **1.a.** 4 groups of 3 =12 **b.** 5 groups of 2=10 **c.** 3,3,3 cakes **1.** December, January, February
Unit 30	**a.** Fifty dollars **b.** five dollars **c.** twenty dollars **d.** ten dollars **e.** one hundred dollars **/ a.** 3 **b.** 5 **c.** 9 **1.a.** 9:30 **b.** 8:00 **c.** 2:30 **2.a.** 6:30 **b.** 5:00 **c.** 11:30 **d.** 7:00 **/ a.** green **b.** blue **c.** black **d.** pink **e.** red